God b

Gary & Valarie Jackson

Maurice Stat

LOOKING UP

when life's got you down

TRUSTING GOD IN THE CRAZY SEASONS OF LIFE

LOOKING UP
when life's got you down
TRUSTING GOD IN THE CRAZY SEASONS OF LIFE

FOREWORD BY
DR. SAMUEL R. CHAND

DR. MAURICE WATSON

Text formatting by Anne McLaughlin of Blue Lake Design, Dickinson, Texas.
Jacket design by Michael Hardie, Atlanta, Georgia.
Published in the United States by Dream Releaser Publishing.

ISBN 978-0-615-40210-9

What leaders are saying about *Looking Up When Life's Got You Down...*

"Everybody goes through hard times, but too many of us fail to trust God in the middle of our "crazy times" in life. In *Looking Up When Life's Got You Down,* Dr. Maurice Watson offers rich, strong encouragement to see difficulties from God's point of view and trust him no matter what. I recommend this book to every person in the family of God."
— Pastor John K. Jenkins, Sr., First Baptist Church of Glenarden, Upper Marlboro, Maryland

"In this powerful and anointed work, Dr. Maurice Watson helps us face the reality of life's down times. He reminds us that each of us inevitably experiences seasons of difficulties. However, he encourages us to remember that our God offers restoration, renewal and revival. We all will be blessed as we dive deep into the spiritual insights of *Looking Up When Life's Got You Down.*"
— Pastor Jeffrey A. Johnson, Sr., Eastern Star Church, Indianapolis, Indiana

"Dr. Maurice Watson is a brilliant expositor of God's word. His message and ministry are powerfully relevant and spiritually reverent. I'm excited about the edification and encouragement that readers will experience as they read this wonderful work."
— Frederick D. Haynes, III, Friendship West Baptist Church, Dallas, Texas

"Maurice Watson is one of the clear, faithful and powerful preaching voices of this generation. It is welcomed news that his dynamic ministry is now extending into print. *Looking Up When Life's Got You Down* inspires all who are facing life's vicissitudes to hope in God. Read it and be blessed. Then bless someone else by getting them a copy of this book."
— Pastor H. B Charles, Jr., Shiloh Metropolitan Baptist Church, Jacksonville, Florida

"Life is full of uncertainties, mysteries and impossibilities. You alone cannot unravel life's 'gordian knot.' In his book, *Looking Up When Life's Got You Down,* Maurice Watson serves as a literary escort taking his readers on a journey toward 'cope-ability.' This book will change the way you see life in the horizontal dimension by affording you with a vertical vision so you can see life from God's point of view."
—Dr. Ralph West, The Church Without Walls, Houston, Texas

I could not have completed this book without the love and support of my wife Janice and our daughters, Marcia and Jessica.

CONTENTS

ACKNOWLEDGEMENTS

I give thanks to the Almighty God for allowing me to complete this book. I hope will bring encouragement to those who read it. I am eternally grateful to my friend, Dr. Samuel Chand, for his guidance and advice throughout this project. I am very grateful to the members of Beulahland Bible Church of Macon/Warner Robins, Georgia, where I Serve as Senior Pastor.

FOREWORD

My friend Dr. Maurice Watson combines the best traits in a pastor. He has a warm, loving, compassionate heart, and he teaches God's Word in a powerful way that changes people's lives. This book contains a wealth of grace and truth, and it imparts insights that help us walk with God through the most difficult seasons of our lives.

We are fallen people living in a fallen world. Things won't be made completely right until we leave this earth and see Christ face to face. For now, we have to struggle against our own sinfulness, the sins of others, all kinds of accidents, unpredictable and sometimes destructive weather, and good-hearted but tragic mistakes that cause us problems. When we expect (or demand!) that God right every wrong, fix every problem, and bless everything we do with success, our unrealistic expectations inevitably lead to disappointment. Let's put it another way: If we begin to try to understand life by looking at the injustice, we will conclude that God doesn't care or that we are so horrible that we deserve harsh punishment. Instead, we need to look first at the sovereignty and goodness of God, at his purposes and processes, and trust that he will use even heartbreak and injustice to accomplish his purposes. In fact, we may see difficult situations as obstacles to avoid or problems to fix, but God sees them in a different light. They are often the very tools God uses to teach us the most valuable lessons. If we resent them, we'll miss those lessons. But if we accept them as lesson plans in the hands of our great and wise Teacher, we will learn wonderful lessons about God, about ourselves, and about life.

Most often, our first reaction to injustice is anger and confusion. And we're not alone. When King David experienced a major setback, he felt God had betrayed him. He was in a panic: "In my alarm I said, 'I am cut off from your sight!' " And at another time when a friend let him down, he gave up on everybody: "And in my dismay I said, 'All men are liars.' " In Psalm 73, Asaph was so upset he felt out of control. He described himself this way,

"Thus my heart was grieved,
And I was vexed in my mind.
I was so foolish and ignorant;
I was like a beast before you." (Psalm 73:21-22).

These are not tepid, shallow emotions expressed by David and Asaph. These feelings are deep, raw, and intense. They are, indeed, normal and obligatory initial reactions to injustice, but they aren't the end of the story.

The psalms are full of honest expressions of joy and grief, thankfulness and bitterness, praise and depression. In almost every psalm in which these complaints are penned, the writer gains insight from God and ends his poem praising God for his wisdom. Even when Asaph was at his worst (acting like "a beast"), God still held his hand. God didn't recoil from him, and he didn't condemn him for struggling with injustice. No, God steadied Asaph, gave him insight, and reassured him of his greatness, love, and sovereignty. Asaph's response to God's grace is one of the most beautiful statements of trust in the Bible. He wrote,

> "Whom have I in heaven but you?
> And there is none upon earth that I desire besides you.
> My flesh and my heart fail;
> But God is the strength of my heart and my portion forever" (Psalm 73:25-26).

Can you identify with Asaph's anger and confusion? If you are alive and if you have noticed the pain and chaos in the world around you, then certainly you have seen your share of heartache. The question is not, "Will God protect us from all injustice?" The experience of injustice is a part of life. Instead, the real question is: "How will we respond to injustice?" and "To whom will I turn for insight when I am angry and confused by it?" We don't know how long Asaph was in the sanctuary before he understood his situation from a higher, eternal, more accurate perspective. We only know he was there long enough so that he didn't miss God's truth.

Not all of our questions, however, will be answered. Asaph received God's perspective about the judgment experienced by prosperous and cocky unbelievers after they die, but he didn't, as far as we know, get any word about why God didn't seem to be blessing his own godliness. But answers to our questions are not as important as this assurance: Even when we don't understand, God does. As long as we have confidence that he is good, he is sovereign, and he is wise, we can trust him. As we'll see in Chapter 1 of this book, in all of Job's suffering, he never blamed God. When he asked God why he had suffered so much, God answered him with a long list of questions to demonstrate his power and authority over all creation and all the affairs of people. With that assurance, Job, like Asaph, worshipped God.

You and I have so much more of the Scriptures than Asaph had. We have far more insight about the will and the ways of God. Let's follow Asaph's example and pursue God's truth and his heart so we, too, have deep understanding about our situations, and like Asaph, a deeper love for God as a result.

To live as victors instead of victims, we need insight about life and God, and we need to muster the courage to take bold action. It helps to have a guide like Dr. Watson to help us on that journey. We need a fresh perspective about the greatness and goodness of our Almighty God. Nothing escapes his notice, and he is willing to use every event, joyful and painful, to accomplish his purposes of deepening our dependence on him. A sense of wonder at God's awesome power and grace stimulates our faith and shapes our responses. Ultimately, however, passive people tend to remain passive, demanding, and fragile . . . until they become convinced that the benefits of change outweigh the benefits of remaining passive and bitter.

We need to rivet our expectations on God—not on him rescuing us out of our problems, but on him graciously using every circumstance and every relationship, self-inflicted wounds and those caused by others, the good we experience as well as the bad, the clear and the confusing, to deepen our dependence on him. That's the message of the Bible, and it's Dr. Watson's message in this book.

Dr. Samuel R. Chand
Atlanta, Georgia
August 2010

CHAPTER 1

A WOUNDED WORSHIPPER

I will lift up my eyes to the hills—
From whence comes my help?
My help comes from the Lord
Who made heaven and earth.
—Psalm 121:1-2

When you're wounded, when life unravels, when your back is against the wall, what do you do? Do you sulk and pout, slip into old habits to block the pain, or wave your fist in the air and curse the heavens? Or do you have a very different response? Do you trust the Lord even when things aren't going well?

God hasn't guaranteed us a life free from difficulties and worry. Our trials and tribulations are decision points in our lives—to trust God more than ever or to turn away from him. Every form of trouble is a test designed by God to strengthen us. In those moments, when the fabric of life unravels and a big problem kicks us to the curb, do we trust him, cling to him, and worship him? One minute, we're one top of the world, but the next, we're struggling for our lives. In the mid-80s, a popular lead singer of a musical group said in a television interview, "Well, you're here today and gone ... later today!" It doesn't take long for life to turn around.

Tests come in all shapes and sizes:

- One moment, life is placid, and the next, it seems to be full of trouble.
- One moment, life is tranquil; the next, it's topsy-turvy.
- One moment, you're on top of the world; the next, it seems you're on the bottom.
- One moment, you have a great job; the next, you're unemployed.
- One moment, you're laughing with joy; the next, you're crying out in pain.
- One moment, your stocks look good and you look forward to retirement, but in a matter of weeks (if not days), your 401-K is only a fraction of its previous worth.

Life can be like that. We can be rocking along, thrilled with our lives and reveling in the wonder of God's blessings, but in the snap of the finger, it could all disappear: your home, your car, your job, your health, your spouse, your children, your wealth, your social status, and even your faith.

TENACIOUS PRAISE

How do we keep from falling apart when our world begins to unravel? That's what we all want to know. The answer is simple and profound: We need to tenaciously praise God. Even in the midst of turmoil, we can choose to be "wounded worshippers." Praising God can get you through even the toughest of times.

The life of Corrie ten Boom demonstrates the incredible power of a praise-filled heart. During the German occupation of the Netherlands in World War II, her family hid Jews from the Nazis in their home in Harlem, but in 1944, the Germans discovered Corrie, her family, and the Jews they were hiding. The soldiers took them to concentration camps. Corrie's book, *The Hiding Place*, graphically describes the horrors of Ravensbruck. As she watched the smoke from the crematorium each day, Corrie knew more innocent people—some who had become friends in the camp—had died a senseless death. Like so many others, Corrie became deeply depressed. Betsie, Corrie's sister, was with her in the camp, and her steadfast faith in God gave Corrie courage. The young women began a secret Bible study in Barracks 28, which became known as "the crazy place, where they hope." Together, they focused their hearts on God's goodness and mercy, even in the darkness of a Nazi death camp. Later, she reflected, "Never be afraid to trust an unknown future to a known God."

Today, we acknowledge Corrie's life as one of faith and hope in the most difficult situation, but she admits that she wouldn't have had faith and hope if they had not been imparted to her by her sister—who soon died in prison. Corrie explained:

> "God has plans—not problems—for our lives. Before she died in the concentration camp in Ravensbruck, my

sister Betsie said to me, 'Corrie, your whole life has been a training for the work you are doing here in prison—and for the work you will do afterward.'

"The life of a Christian is an education for higher service. No athlete complains when the training is hard. He thinks of the game, or the race. Looking back across the years of my life, I can see the working of a divine pattern which is the way of God with His children. When I was in a prison camp in Holland during the war, I often prayed, 'Lord, never let the enemy put me in a German concentration camp.' God answered no to that prayer. Yet in the German camp, with all its horror, I found many prisoners who had never heard of Jesus Christ.

"If God had not used my sister Betsie and me to bring them to Him, they would never have heard of Him. Many died, or were killed, but many died with the name of Jesus on their lips. They were well worth all our suffering. Faith is like radar which sees through the fog—the reality of things at a distance that the human eye cannot see."[1]

At times when we want to run away and hide, we can learn some valuable lessons from an Old Testament hero. For most Christians, the book of Job is a favorite story in the Bible. We often turn to this story when we find ourselves in the midst of the unexplainable and unbearable. The message of Job a source of strength and encouragement when our lives have unraveled and come apart. Though it was probably the first piece of

Scripture ever penned and was written thousands of years ago, the book provides solace for those today who are facing life's most difficult trials. The message has lifted people's spirits when they, like Job, are lying on their own beds of affliction.

Job offers us valuable insights about God, our situations, and ourselves when life makes no sense. At the beginning of the saga, Job was fabulously rich. He had seven sons, three daughters, seven thousand sheep, three thousand camels, five hundred yoke of oxen, five hundred donkeys, and a large number of servants. In one day, however, he lost them all. When he heard the tragic news, he was heartbroken. He grieved the pain and loss, but he held tight to his trust in the goodness and greatness of God. He steadfastly refused to blame God for his problems. In Job 1:22, the narrative says, "In all this, Job did not sin by charging God with wrongdoing."

What would you do?

Job was the wealthiest man of his time, but most importantly, he was a man of faith. Having faith in God doesn't exempt us from facing the trials of life. In fact, strong faith invites the enemy's attacks. When we've proven that we love God with all our hearts and are willing to obey him through thick and thin, Satan will come after us with even more vengeance because we're a threat to him. Though Job was a man of faith, he faced one tragic moment after another. His faith was no guarantee of safety, security, peace, and continued prosperity.

Do you remember how his trouble began? The Bible says in Job 1:6-10 (with a touch of paraphrase), "When the sons of

God came to present themselves before the Lord, Satan came among them also. And God said to the devil, 'Satan, where have you been?'"

Satan told God, "I've been up and down, to and fro, seeking whom I may devour."

God asked, "Satan, have you considered my servant, Job? He's an upstanding, righteous man; a man who fears God and loves the Lord and eschews evil."

Satan responded, "Well, I thought about Job, but I gave up on him. I decided not to bother Job, and the reason is that you blessed him too much."

Satan continued the conversation by offering a wager: "You see, God, that's why Job is serving you. I mean, who wouldn't serve you if they had all of what Job has? You have blessed him incredibly! He's got it made; that's why he serves you. But I'll tell you what, if you let me take his possessions away from him, I'll show you what your servant Job is made of. When your blessings are gone, he'll turn his back on you. He'll curse you to your face!"

And God said, "All right, Devil. I'm going to take you up on your offer."

Satan was under the misguided assumption that Job worshiped God only because God had blessed him with many possessions and comforts. Satan didn't understand that Job worshiped God because he loved him, no matter how much or how little God blessed him. God answered, "Devil, you can touch everything in Job's life. But whatever you do, don't touch his soul or kill him, because his soul belongs to me."

That's how it started. Years of blessings were taken away in a flash on a single tragic day. Job had many questions about his painful losses, but he never gave up on God. Nearly 3,000 years later, we can learn from Job how to tenaciously cling to God when things go bad.

When Job heard the series of reports of unspeakable calamities, he turned his thoughts toward God. The narrator tells us, "At this, Job got up and tore his robe and shaved his head. Then he fell to the ground in worship." In the ancient world, tearing a robe was a common practice for those in mourning. It was their way of saying, "My torn garment is a symbol of how my soul has been torn to pieces." Also, shaving the head was a common practice for those mourning the loss of a loved one. A male would shave his head and sit in sackcloth and ashes. He threw ashes in the air, allowing his body to be covered in soot and ashes as a way of saying, "I am in deep mourning."

Last, but most importantly, Job fell to the ground and worshipped God. He had lost all of his wealth, camels, sheep and all ten of his children. I don't know about you, but losing one child would crush me. I would fall to the ground, too, in anguish and pain. He lost all ten on one day. His pain must have been incomprehensible. When I studied this passage, I noticed something important about Job's fall to the ground—it was not a spontaneous, involuntary reaction. He didn't lose control of his body and collapse in a heap when he heard the horrific news that day. He didn't lose the strength in his legs, and his knees didn't buckle because of the loss. Instead, he fell intentionality to the ground with the sole purpose of worshipping God.

Can you image that? Can you imagine what it would be like to lose your job, and the first thing you do is raise your hands to heaven and worship our Heavenly Father? Or lose a child, or hear the diagnosis of cancer, or hear about a terrible car wreck, or any other tragic news? Job fell to the ground, not to curl up in the fetal position in bitterness, anger, or thoughts of suicide. He fell to the ground and worshipped God!

To respond to tragedy with this measure of great faith, we *must*—and I suggest *must* because it's imperative to respond this way—turn our thoughts from our trouble and look up toward God. If we, like Job, "can just get a glimpse of God," reflect on his incomparable goodness, and see life from the divine perspective, we can make it through any crisis. It may feel terrible, and we may grieve for a long time, but it won't crush our spirits.

We can get through all kinds of heartaches and disappointments when we stop looking *down* and stop looking *around*, but start looking *up* to the Lord. We have to get outside ourselves. Job didn't turn his thoughts inwardly or outwardly. He turned his thoughts upwardly. Someone has observed that sorrow looks back and worry looks around, but faith looks up.

If you're going to stay strong in times of trouble, you've got to bow your heart down and lift your eyes up. In Psalm 121:1-2, the psalmist says, "I will lift up my eyes to the hills—

From whence comes my help? My help comes from the Lord, who made heaven and earth." And Psalm 24:7 says, "Lift up your heads, O you gates! And be lifted up, you everlasting doors! And the King of glory shall come in." These two verses remind us to look up, even in the down times of life. When life falls apart, choose to worship God. Turn your thoughts toward God because worship is an antidote for a host of stress-related reactions, including depression, hopelessness, thoughts of suicide, and manic activity. You won't lose your mind—you won't go crazy and fall apart—if you choose to worship God.

If, however, you focus only on the depth of your problems, you just might lose your mind. You might lay awake at night worrying, walk around depressed, or begin to lose touch with reality. However, if you can get your mind off the problems and focus your attention on God, you *will* make it. If Job can, you can, too.

THANKING GOD NO MATTER WHAT

Job did more than fall to the ground in a heap of grief. When he fell to the ground, he worshiped God. And when he turned his thoughts toward his Heavenly Father, he did one more thing: He thanked God. Even in his deepest pain and darkest moment, Job chose to thank God for his goodness and greatness. In verse 21 we read, "Naked I came from my mother's womb, and naked shall I return there. The Lord gave, and the Lord has taken away; blessed be the name of the Lord."

What a lesson Job teaches us today! We can learn from him that no matter how bad things are, we can always find a reason to give God the praise he so richly deserves. The word *blessed* literally means "to speak well of." In essence, Job says, "I'm going to speak well of God. I lost everything, but I'm not going to curse God. Instead, I'm going to thank him. I'm going to choose to bless God."

When times are tough, you can't have "little boy faith" that runs away at the first sign of trouble. You need faith like Job when he said, despite all his calamities, "Blessed be the name of the Lord." God is waiting on us to express this kind of faith to him. He waits on us to grow up so we can find out that he's good—not only when he gives you a new house, but he is good while you watch that house burn to the ground. God is good when he gives you a car, and he's still good when you have to catch the bus because your car breaks down. God is good when you're healthy, but he's good when the dreaded diagnosis comes back that you have cancer.

Are you capable of saying, "Thank you, Lord!" during your times of trouble? Will you praise the Lord if you don't get the house, the nice car you want, or the dream job? If you can't, Satan wins. When things go awry, "the enemy of our souls" wants you to walk away from God and lose your desire to praise God. Don't let him win. The thing Satan wanted most was for Job to blame God. He wanted Job to wallow in self-pity and to doubt the love and sovereignty of God. The enemy still uses this tactic on us today. He tries to make us feel that God has turned his back on us, or that we must have done something wrong for God to allow calamity in our lives.

Instead, like Job, we need to find something for which to thank God because, as bad as things are, they could always be a whole lot worse. If you are dealing with a lost job, think about the person who hasn't eaten in a week. If you lost your home through a foreclosure, think about the homeless person living under the bridge. Someone once said, "I complained that I had no shoes until I saw a man who had no feet." No matter how bad life is, it could always be worse.

Paul wrote to the Christians in Thessalonica, "In everything give thanks, for this is the will of God in Christ Jesus concerning you." He doesn't say, "In everything *feel* thankful." That is a huge difference. Thanksgiving is not a feeling; it's an action. In spite of everything that may be going wrong, decide to thank God. When you are able to make this choice, you know you're growing in your walk with God. You may not have the perfect marriage, but you can still thank God for your spouse. Your children may get in trouble every now and then, but you can still thank God for them. You may not have the amount of money in your bank account that you wish, but you can still thank God for what he has entrusted to you.

You can make the decision to give God praise and thanksgiving for what he has given you—and he has given you everything. It's not a right to have all your talents, time, and treasure. You would have nothing without his grace and his mercy, and so, if you lose it all, you're back to even. That's why Job could say, "Naked I came into the world, and naked shall I return. The Lord gave and the Lord has taken away, and the answer is this: Blessed be the name of the Lord."

"YET PRAISE"

Are you at the place in your walk that you can praise God in spite of what you're going through? I call that a "yet praise." There's trouble all around, "yet I'll praise God." Despite the trials in my life, "yet I'll praise the Lord." I have no money in the bank, "yet I'll praise him." I'm sick, "yet I'll praise God anyway." Praise and gratitude bring joy that that money can't buy, water can't drown, cold can't freeze, and nothing can destroy.

When we choose to trust God no matter what, we can be wounded and still worship. Somebody said. "When praises go up, blessings come down." Sometimes it just takes a minute. We take coffee breaks, so why not stop and take a praise break? You might be surprised at how much better you'll feel. Praise taps into the heart of God, connects us with his goodness and mercy, and rekindles our faith so that we trust him even more and experience his peace.

When you suffer life's discouragements or tragedies, don't forget about Job and what he did when his life fell apart: He turned his heart toward God, thanked him, and refreshed his faith in thoughts about the majesty and grace of God. Job said, "Though he slay me, though he kill me, though he causes me pain, though he causes me to die, yet will I trust him." Job wondered if God was causing his pain, but even then, he decided to cling to God. He said, "Even if God kills me, I've decided I'm going to trust him."

The issue is not "why bad things happen to good people," but this: Can we trust God when he allows the worst to happen to us? Can we still trust him when he allows a loved one to die? Can we have confidence in him when he allows us to be laid off from a job? Can our faith remain strong when we find out we have a terrible disease?

As we read the story of Job, we get a glimpse into a painful moment when the one person still alive and near him has given up on God—and has given up on Job. In the middle of all his pain, his wife asked, "Why don't you curse God and die?"

I can hear Job responding to her, "Yes, dear, I know. I lost it all. Here is where I stand. No matter what, I'm sticking with God." He replied, "Though he slay me, yet will I trust him." Job's faith was unshakeable. He was a deeply wounded man, but he expressed his trust and his confidence in God.

When life falls apart and life begins to unravel, we need the kind of robust faith that rivets our hearts on God's character and sees us through. Flimsy faith will always fail. Shallow, superficial faith won't do. The kind of trust that only exists when times are good will desert us when we need it most. We need a strong, mature faith that will enable us to trust God, even when life itself is coming unglued. That requires a deeper faith:

- A faith that will hold you when the stormy winds of life are blowing,
- A faith that will stabilize you when you are about to fall,
- A faith that will help you to say with new meaning, "I have decided to follow Jesus. I've made up my mind—no turning back," and

- A faith that will help you to hold on when everything in your life says you ought to give up and let go.

That's the kind of faith I want, and that's the kind I need. It's the kind that helps me say about God, "Although he slay me, yet will I trust him. In spite of my pain, I'm still going to praise him. I may be wounded, but my wounds won't stop my worship."

Are you able, are you strong enough, do you have enough faith to worship God in spite of your pain? Can you lift your eyes and your heart to God? If I can get a glimpse of God's love, his mercy, his wisdom, and his power, I can make it through the storm. If I can just enter into the presence of the Lord, I'll keep from losing my mind.

Having trials and tribulations is a part of being human—a common lot we all share. Down times are inescapable realities of life. If we live long enough, life has a way of falling apart, sometimes suddenly and swiftly. But as we have learned from Job, the next time something doesn't go our way, no matter how little or big, we can make the first thought praise to God. We may be wounded, but we can still be worshippers.

CHAPTER 2

THE TESTIMONY OF A SURVIVOR

Many are the afflictions of the righteous,

But the Lord delivers him out of them all.

—Psalm 34:19

In the early part of this millennium, Survivor became one of the most popular shows on television. Now regarded as the mother of American reality shows, the program pits a group of stranded strangers in a remote location and forces them to battle for food, water, fire, and shelter. The winner of the marathon series of contests receives $1 million. Anyone who has watched the show knows that contestants often resort to any tactic to advance in the game. They lie, steal, betray, and backstab others in pursuit of the grand prize.

In real life, people often use the same tactics to survive. That's why the phrases "dog eat dog," "whatever it takes," and "kick 'em while they're down" are motivating mantras for some. However, God has provided quite different ways for Christians to survive—and in fact, thrive. It's not necessary to lie, steal, betray, and backstab. Instead of competing and trying to beat each other, we can learn to love and affirm each other. We can live according to God's grace, love, and glory. In each trial or tribulation, we can choose how we want to deal with adversity.

THE MYSTERIES OF LIFE

When we hear about people's painful experiences, we often shake our heads in wonder. Sometimes, tragedies make no sense at all. For instance,

- One person is involved in a violent automobile accident but walks away unscathed. Another is involved in a less violent accident but is paralyzed.
- One person faces a devastating loss but finds hope in the midst of pain. Another goes into a deep depression.
- One person goes through a divorce and learns valuable lessons from the heartache. Another goes through a divorce and becomes angry, cynical, and bitter.
- One person loses a job but trusts in the faithfulness of God for a better one. Another loses a job and sees only a mountain of financial despair.
- One person loses a loved one but reflects often of the good times they shared. Another loses a loved one and gives up on God and life.

It's not *what* happens to you, but *how* you respond that really matters. In each of those situations, the person had a choice to trust God or give up. The word *trust* means "to seek shelter and to seek refuge in." To whom, or to what, do you turn for refuge in times of trouble? Where do you seek shelter in your times of storms? Some people turn to alcohol, and others seek comfort from a crack pipe. Some turn to their bank account, and others rely on family and friends. Some bolt to the shopping mall, and others numb the pain by devouring tremendous amounts of comfort food. In one way or another, many people depend on their own strength.

However, the testimony of countless people is this: None of that will work. Self-effort and escape may promise instant relief, but they ultimately let us down and leave us in despair. Put away the pitiful pride, and throw aside self-absorbed anger. The only person we can trust without fear of being let down is God. Trust in God . . . completely . . . totally . . . with all your heart. Anyone who trusts in God will not be condemned or disappointed. The psalmist wrote, "God is our refuge and strength, a very present help in the time of trouble." His testimony reminds us where we ought to turn.

The opening lines of Gloria Gaynor's 1979 hit song, "I Will Survive" said, "First I was afraid; I was petrified." If you completely trust God, you won't be afraid or petrified. You will have peace—complete and comforting peace. With God's peace, you'll understand that whatever comes your way won't destroy you. It may damage you, and it may hurt, but in the long run, it's much like a flesh wound. It hurts very badly, but it doesn't do lasting damage. You have the ability to get through it.

Have you gone through something like that? A horrible car accident? Divorce? The death of a family member or best friend? A debilitating disease? Betrayal by someone you respected? All of us have suffered, but not all of us have trusted God in our pain. No one has been through life unscathed. All of us have endured our share of dire circumstances. If you are a survivor, and you trusted God to give you strength in the storm, you have a testimony. Share it with people. As the saying goes, "We experience to equip." Your testimony will help others through their rough patches of life.

The testimony of believers in every era, from Job to today, shows us: Living right doesn't guarantee a trouble-free life, but we need to trust God with all our hearts, and we also need the right resources to survive. Living right or being religious is no guarantee you will skate through without facing any trouble. Unfortunately, many believe that being right with God will shield them from times of trouble and heartache. This is a common misconception, particularly of new believers who haven't been taught about God's school of testing. The truth is that trouble is an inevitable reality in this life. There's no way around it. You can't hide from it. You can't run from it. Trouble is coming your way. The old folks used to say it like this: "If you haven't had any trouble, just keep living, 'cause trouble's got your address. Sooner or later, he's coming to your house."

You can expect to face a lot of trouble in life. If you haven't, you will. Whether or not you are a believer, trouble will find you. That's just a fact of life. You might face trouble in the home, with your finances, with sickness, or with your children. Sooner or later, trouble will knock on your door. Will you be prepared?

THE SUFFERING OF THE RIGHTEOUS

The story of King David is a good reminder that living right doesn't guarantee us a life free from trouble. David was "a man after God's own heart," yet he still faced horrific problems. He survived by pushing through the pain and not beating himself up over it. When we struggle, it's wise to look in the mirror to see if we caused it or contributed to it in any way. If we did, we need to be honest and repent. If not, we need to accept the situation as God's graduate school of spiritual development. Don't beat yourself over the head when you're going through uncomfortable times. Suffering doesn't necessarily mean that you must have done something wrong or that you must have made God mad. No, sometimes when you're in the right, trouble still comes.

Job said it like this in 14:1: "Man that is born of a woman is of a few days, and those few days are full of trouble." Not only are troubles inevitable, but they are also innumerable. David points out, "Many are the afflictions of the righteous." The word *many* means "great in number." Even for the righteous, afflictions abound.

Look at some of the things David endured:

- As a boy he faced a nine-foot giant named Goliath.
- As a boy he endured the anger of King Saul, who got

jealous of him and tried to kill him. Consequently, David suffered while hiding in caves in the wilderness.

- He was captured and thrown in prison.
- When he became an adult, a man ran away with one of his wives.
- His wife Micah despised him.
- One of his sons, Amnon, raped his daughter Tamar.
- Absalom, another son, killed Amnon for the rape.
- Absalom tried to overthrow his father from the throne.

David endured a lot of trouble, but he survived. In his story we also see that trouble doesn't discriminate. We may hope that trouble only finds those who we think deserve it. Remember what David wrote, "Many are the afflictions of the righteous." If I had written that verse, it would read, "Many are the afflictions *of the wicked*." Or, "Many are the afflictions *of gangbangers*." Maybe I would write it this way, "Many are the afflictions *of criminals and mean people*." We expect people who live those lifestyles to face trouble, but David reveals that trouble pays no heed to race, color, social status, or belief-system. You can have a right standing with God—that's what "righteousness" means—and still get sick, laid off from your job, or have your spouse leave you. Jesus said in John 16:33, "In the world, you will have tribulation; but be of good cheer, I have overcome the world."

We also learn from David's story that we need to trust in the faithfulness of God. His life and language tell us, "We can count on a harsh reality: Trouble is going to come. But a greater reality is that God will remain faithful to deliver us." In the middle of that verse is the crucial word "but." That's a holy conjunction. That one tiny word carries a lot of weight and takes the sting out of the previous statement. "But" provides hope so you have something to hold onto and not lose your mind.

Also, in that verse we find the word *delive*r, which means "to snatch, to snatch up, to rescue." The word *deliver* is used in the imperfect tense. Perfect tense refers to a completed action, but imperfect tense refers to an action that occurred in the past, is still happening right now, and will be completed in the future. When David says, "God delivers him," it's in the imperfect tense, which means that while your deliverance is not complete, it is already in process. God's promise is that you will make it through whatever you are enduring, whatever has come against you. That's his promise: You will survive. It may not look like it, but his action to rescue you is already in process. You may not see any signs that things are getting any better, but your deliverance is coming.

Abraham was told by God to take his son, Isaac, to the land of Moriah and kill him on an altar on the mountain. In a great act of faith, Abraham obeyed. The Bible says he took him to Mt. Moriah, tied up the boy's hands and feet, laid him on the altar, and drew back his knife to kill him. And just about the time he was about to bring that knife down to kill him, God told an angel, "Get down there!" I imagine the angel flew quicker than it ever had flown before! Before the knife fell, the angel told Abraham, "Do not lay your hand on the lad, or do anything to him; for now I know that you fear God, since you have not withheld your son, your only son, from me." Abraham lifted his eyes and looked behind him to find a ram that was caught in a thicket by its horns. The ram became a substitute that died in the place of his Isaac.

The Bible doesn't say this, but I believe that when Abraham and Isaac went up one side of the mountain, the ram went up the other side. When the problem went up one side, the answer went up the other side. What you need to survive is already on the way to your rescue, just like the ram was coming to take Isaac's place. You may be sick, but healing is on the way. Your finances might be suffering, but you can be assured that everything will be all right. Whatever it is, doors may not be open yet, but they will be.

We survive because God is faithful. And because God is faithful, we know our deliverance has already been set in motion. The wounds we suffer are temporary. David explains: "He guards all his bones, not one of them is broken." There's a difference between being wounded—a flesh wound—and a broken bone. Broken bones are deep on the inside. With a flesh wound you can still function. Understand what is being said here. In tumultuous times God protects our bones. We may get bruised and wounded, but even if we are bruised on the outside, God won't let us be broken on the inside. If we trust God, our spirit can't be broken. God will allow us to be wounded, but we'll still be able to function. You might have trouble all around, but if you trust in God's eventual provision, you'll have hope.

This kind of inner strength will get you through a lot of trouble. Why is it that trouble causes some to become *better* but causes others to become *bitter*? I believe it has something to do with our value system. David draws a contrast between how the righteous respond and are affected by trouble with how the wicked respond and are affected by trouble. He says, "Evil shall slay the wicked, and those who hate the righteous shall be condemned."

The word *evil* is the same word for affliction in a previous verse, "Many are the afflictions of the righteous." Here we have two people who go through the same trouble, and yet they have very different outcomes. One is able to survive, and the other is shattered.

- The righteous are delivered, but the wicked are destroyed.
- The righteous are protected, but the wicked suffer harm.
- The righteous are vindicated, but the wicked are condemned.
- The righteous are made better, but the wicked become bitter.

Why do some people praise God in spite of their trouble, while others curse God? When we go through trouble, we've got a God that we can lean on. However, when the wicked encounter trouble, they don't have a God to lean on. What do we know about God and his purposes for our pain?

- We know that "greater is he that is in us, than he that is in the world."
- We know that "all things work together for the good of those who love the Lord."
- We know that "the joy of the Lord is our strength."
- We know that if we wait on the Lord, "he will renew our strength, and we will mount up with wings as eagles. We will run and not be weary; we'll walk and not faint."
- We understand that "many are the afflictions of the righteous, but the Lord delivers him from them all."

Here's the bottom line: David reminds us, "Do not fret because of evildoers, nor be envious of the workers of iniquity. For they shall soon be cut down like the grass and wither as the green herb" (Psalm 37:1-2). You can be sure that payday is coming for the people who sent you through hell, the people that lied to your face or behind your back, and the ones who rejoiced at your suffering. They may have tried to wipe you out, but they are the ones who will be wiped out.

The last thing we learn from David's story is to have the right resources. Tapping into the wrong resource can be fatal. The Lord redeems the soul of his servant. The word *redeem* means "to vindicate, to restore to a place of honor." It is the idea of a slave who is bought out of slavery, set free, and restored to a place of honor.

KEEP PRAYING AND PRAISING

Make up your mind that you'll pray until your deliverance comes. When praises go up, blessings come down. Be glad that you can testify that you're a survivor. Just like you, I've made it through some rough times in my life. Sometimes we feel like praising and thanking God, but true faith is revealed when we praise and thank him before he delivers us—and even if he doesn't deliver us. In the ancient kingdom of Babylon, three faithful young men—Shadrach, Meshach, and Abednego—faced the choice of renouncing God or being thrown into Nebuchadnezzar's fiery furnace, they replied calmly and boldly, "O Nebuchadnezzar, we have no need to answer you in this matter. If that is the case, our God whom we serve is able to deliver us from the burning fiery furnace, and He will deliver us from your hand, O king. But if not, let it be known to you, O king, that we do not serve your gods, nor will we worship the gold image which you have set up" (Daniel 3:16-18).

You know the story. The furious king heated the oven so hot that his soldiers burned to death just by standing near it. When they threw the three men into the fire, the Lord appeared with them and protected them. They were determined to be faithful no matter what the outcome might be, but God chose to honor their faith by delivering them. In the same way, God wants us to demonstrate our trust in him by praising him—even when we don't see his deliverance yet. When we fill our hearts with thoughts of his wonder, strength, and grace, amazing things happen. Praising God runs the demons away. It makes the drugs become distasteful. It brings marriages back together. It brings children back home. It makes your enemies leave you alone.

God, and only God, can restore us. Everything else will let us down. People will count you out and say you're not going to make it, but just take a look at yourself. You have weathered the storm. Sing and dance, not just in celebration, but also to become a survivor in life.

CHAPTER 3

I'VE GOT A FEELING

All hope that we would be saved was finally given up. — Acts 27:20

At some point in your life—maybe even this week or possibly today—you've probably felt like giving up. The pressures you endured have multiplied, and you lost hope. You wanted to throw in the proverbial towel, or maybe you just wanted to sit and have a good cry.

Have you ever been there? Have you ever faced those moments in life when you felt that going on was completely useless? You may have believed that you wouldn't be able to make it through the tough time you were experiencing. The next step seemed to take you into an abyss of despair.

HONESTY: THE DOOR TO HOPE

If we're honest, we'd all have to say "yes" to these questions at some point in our lives. The causes are as varied as our individual stories. We may have lost a job, a parent, a friend, a spouse, or a in Nebraska, I had to catch a plane to Wichita, Kansas, to preach. Most of the flight was very smooth, exactly how most of us like it, but suddenly, the pilot announced urgently, "Flight attendants, take your seats immediately! I want everybody to fasten your seatbelts really tight because in a few minutes, we're going to hit some exceptionally bad turbulence."

When a pilot tells me—at thirty-five thousand feet and five hundred miles an hour—to sit down and buckle my seatbelt, I'm not going to argue with him! I sat down and pulled the strap until I could barely breathe! Only minutes later, we hit the worst turbulence I had ever experienced in all my years of flying. The plane instantly dropped several feet, finishing with a jolt and a bang. Some people screamed. Others white-knuckled their armrests.

I cried out, "O God! Please keep us, please!"

The pilot came on the intercom again to explain that we were out of the layer of disturbed air. From the tone of his voice, I could tell that he wasn't afraid. Do you know why? He knew that no matter how bumpy it got, the plane would be able to handle the turbulence. A few minutes later, he began the descent, and we landed safely.

The principle applies to us in our turbulent lives. No matter how bumpy a ride you're on with your finances, health, relationships, or work, it's not time to quit or give up in despair. It's just a bumpy ride. Our Pilot knows what he's doing, he has plenty of experience, and he knows the skies and the plane very well. We can trust him to see us through the problems.

If we'll listen to his instructions and fasten our seatbelts, we can hold on, wait on God to work, and trust that he'll lead us to safety—in his way and in his timing. Isaiah tells us, "But those who wait on the Lord shall renew their strength" (Isaiah 40:31). If we listen, trust, wait, and hold on, it's going to be all right. Life can be very bumpy, but things smooth out after a while.

TAKING OFF THE MASK

In moments of despair when our hope wavers, we must be careful to recognize the painful principle: "Misery loves company." Some people are downers, and their attitudes poison everyone who comes near them. They may not mean to ruin our perspective, but their unresolved past wounds color their thinking and cause them to be sour, negative, and full of doubts. We need to find people who have a track record of trusting God in hard times. We can learn a lot from them. They're out there, but they're often quiet men and women who have been tempered in the hot fire of trials. Their faith is strong, but they don't advertise the school where they've learned their most cherished lessons. When times are hard, we desperately need the input and affirmation of people who have been through life's fires and have come out like tempered steel.

Have you ever gone to church to seek a word from God, but you didn't want anyone to know you were in need? You hid begin a mask that said, "I'm doing just fine, thank you." You were looking good and smelling good, a smile on your face, hallelujahs on your lips, and your hands lifted up in praise. But if the truth were told, behind all of your smiles, behind all of your hand waving, and behind all of your hallelujahs, you'd decided, "If I don't get a word today from the Lord, I don't think I'm going to be able to make it. I don't know if I can make it till next Sunday, or even tomorrow. I'm dying inside!"

A lay leader of a prominent church in Texas was widely respected for his dedication to the ministry, but on a retreat with the pastoral staff and elders, he had a seizure and fell into a lake. Another man jumped into the water and held his head up until others came to drag him out of the water. When EMS came, they asked if he had been drinking. The rest of the people around him laughed at the thought. They couldn't imagine that could be the problem. After a night in the hospital, however, the truth came out. He had been an alcoholic for years, but he had kept it a secret from everyone at the church. His wife knew, but like many codependents, she denied the reality of his problem. For him, "the rest of the story" is a magnificent tale of refreshing honesty, healing, and redemption. He went into rehab, carved out a new lifestyle, and now is a leader of recovery ministries at the church. As he looks back on his life, he reflects, "For years, I lived a lie. No one knew but me—or so I thought. God knew, and he wasn't willing for me to keep living the lie any longer. He finally got my attention. I wish I'd responded to his nudging and whispers all those years, but I didn't. It took a sledgehammer to get my attention. Change didn't happen until I was willing to be honest."

Until we take off our masks, we won't find the help we need. Until we're honest about the pain we feel, we won't find comfort. As long as we insist on hiding and playing games, we block the flow of love and insight that can come from those around us who have learned the lessons we desperately need to learn. The reality is that there are people all around us who need to learn those lessons, too. They face their own world of debilitating hurts and shattered hopes. We need the Body of Christ to be led by the Spirit of God to bring light into our darkness, and then we can carry God's light to others who are struggling through dark times.

To learn the lessons God wants to teach us in times of testing and trial, we need to see beyond the immediate problem to grasp God's deeper purpose for our lives. In his book *Reaching for the Invisible God*, Philip Yancey explains, "Gregory of Nicea once called St. Basil's faith 'ambidextrous' because he welcomed pleasures with the right hand and afflictions with the left, convinced both would serve God's design for him."[2] When we have deeper, richer insight about the purposes of God, we gain "ambidextrous faith," trusting God in the good times and the bad to teach us valuable lessons and shape us into the image of Christ.

PARTNERS FROM PARADISE

How do you deal with the disappointments and hopelessness of life? How do you encourage others going through struggles? We need to understand that when we go through storms in life, some angelic partners from paradise come to our rescue. We don't have to lose hope. We need to understand that we aren't alone. Angels were, and still are, special messengers of God—superhuman, immortal beings who are servants of God. They are God's messengers who run the errands of the Most High. Angels are very common in Scripture. Almost every book in the Bible mentions them. In fact, with the exception of Ruth, Nehemiah, Esther, the epistles of John, and the epistle of James, every other book in the Bible describes the existence and ministry of angels. Paul tells a group of hopeless men who were in the midst of a storm and doubted they were going to come out of it, "Men . . . I urge you to take heart, for there will be no loss of life among you, but only of the ship. For there stood by me this night an angel of the God to whom I belong and whom I serve" (Acts 27:21-23).

Angels carry the message of God and serve the purposes of God. Since they are the servants of God, they are also friends of God's children, you and me. When you and I go through storms in life, angelic partners from paradise stand ready to come to our rescue. We may feel alone, but God and his angels never abandon us. They're here, around us right now, to protect us, care for us, and provide for us.

Throughout the Bible, we find that when times got tough for the children of God, an angel often came to the rescue. When Lot was in Sodom and Gomorrah and needed deliverance, an angel rescued him and his family. When

Balaam was about to curse the people of God and lead them into sin, an angel stood in his path with a sword drawn, and the mule on which Balaam rode began to talk. When God wanted to tell Mary that she would be the mother of the Messiah, he sent an angel to give her the message. When Jesus was tempted in the desert, angels came to minister to him. The list goes on and on. When life becomes dark and dismal, know that you are not alone.

Angels strengthen our faith by reminding us of God's character, and they often use the truth of God's Word to put steel in our souls. The doctor may have given you bad news, but stand firm and believe the Word of God. An employer may have said he isn't hiring right now, but stand and believe the Word of God. There's never been a problem that God couldn't solve. He is a winning God. The "game" may look hopelessly lost, but God is the master of comebacks! He won at the Red Sea, and he won at the walls of Jericho. He won at Daniel's lion den, he won at the fiery furnace, and he won at the wedding at Cana when the wine ran out. He won at Jairus' house when his daughter died. He won in the city of Nain when the widow's son had died, and he won again at the grave of Lazarus, who had been dead for four days when the Lord shouted, "Lazarus, come forth!"

One dark Friday, they hung Jesus high, stretched him wide, and dropped him low—and he died. He died till the sun wouldn't shine. He died until the moon dripped down in blood. He died until the earth was reeling and rocking like a drunken man. But early Sunday morning, Jesus won again. He got up with all power in his hand. The forces of darkness thought they had won, but on that morning, light shattered the darkness! The story of God's work in the world assures us, "Be not dismayed for whatever betide you, God will take care of you."

With the assurance of the resurrection and the stories of God's miracles, why should we feel discouraged? Why do we let the shadows come in and block out the light of God's love, hope, and joy? Why should our hearts feel lonely and afraid? As we think about the track record of God's faithfulness and power, we can almost hear Jesus saying the words to us that he said to the doubting disciples in the boat after he calmed the storm, "Where is your faith?"

What should be the response of one who is facing insurmountable odds with seemingly no way in sight for him to overcome those odds? We can follow the example of great people who give us hope. We can look at Jesus, "the author and perfector of our faith." And we can read the stories of the heroes of the faith listed in Hebrews 11 and throughout the Bible. Some of us draw motivation and hope from today's athletes like Derek Jeter or Michael Jordan, or from real-life heroes such as fireman, policeman, and soldiers. In addition to following the example of others, biblical principles give us courage when we feel like giving up.

Paul spent more than two years in prison because of false accusations against him by those who hated him and wanted to kill him. In that dire situation, he invoked his Roman citizenship by appealing to have his case tried before Caesar in Rome. In Acts 27, Paul boarded a ship laden with cargo and 275 other prisoners, guards, and officials, and they set sail for Rome. At first, the sailing was smooth and serene, but as the voyage went on, a fierce storm rocked the ship. The wind began to roar; it blew madly out of control, howling like a maniac! The sea, which at first provided smooth sailing, became angry and began to rock the ship, tossing and turning it like a drunken man. With one hand, the sea made a fist and pounded the ship broadside. With the other hand, the sea grabbed the ship and used it as if it were a dipper, filling it with salty and foamy raging water. The thunder began to roar like a hundred hungry, vicious lions, and the lightening flashed across the sky, causing the sky to appear as if it were on fire for a few brief moments. The brilliant light of the sun was hidden behind the opaque, dark clouds, causing the atmosphere to be as dark as a thousand midnights.

In the middle of these terrible, dark, foreboding circumstances, Luke describes the scene: "Now when neither sun nor stars appeared for many days, and no small tempests beat on us, all hope that we would be saved was finally given up." The men had given up hope they would ever reach the shore alive. They didn't see any way for them to make it out of this situation, but God intervened, sending an angel to assure Paul that he would, in fact, make it to Rome to plead his case before Caesar. Relaying the angel's message to the soldiers and prisoners on the ship, Paul told them, "Men, I know it looks bad. I know it seems as if we're not going to make it out of this. I know the wind is blowing and the sea is contrary, and I know it seems as if all hope is lost." But he said, "Men, don't concentrate on the circumstances. I refuse to believe my circumstance because my circumstance can lie to me. Rather, I believe God." He assured them, "Therefore, men, take heart, for I believe God that it will be just as it was told me."

You may assume there's no way out of your predicament. Your sad and discouraged heart may tell you that your trouble is going to last forever, but God said, "Weeping may endure suffering for a night, but joy will come in the morning." Your circumstances may be telling you God is not going to answer your prayer, but God said, "They that wait on the Lord shall renew their strength, they shall mount up with wings as eagles, they shall run and not be weary, they shall walk and not faint."

When storms blow in your life, you can say like Paul, "But I believe God." That's how you deal with a hopeless hour. You can say to yourself, your family, and everyone who will listen, "I believe God. I know the circumstances seem terrible, but that's all right. I still believe God."

Our president has the best protection of any person on the face of the earth. He has Secret Service protection twenty-four hours a day, three hundred sixty-five days a year. In spite of that fact, presidents have been shot and others have been assassinated. Secret Service protection is the finest in the world, but it's not foolproof. God's protection for us, though, is even better than the Secret Service. We've got angelic protection. The old folks of my childhood used to say it like this: "It's all night, and it's all day, that the angels keep watching over me."

I've driven through red lights and gotten three blocks on the other side before I realized that I ran the light. I could have killed myself or killed others, but God protected us. The angels were watching over me. Quite often when I've been tempted to sin, the angels said, "No, you don't! Stay away from there!" Sometimes I've wanted to go in a certain direction, but God knew better. He sent his angels to tell me, "Don't go that way. Go this way."

A CLEAR AND STRONG IDENTITY

What should be the response of one who is facing insurmountable odds with apparently no way in sight to overcome those odds? Maybe you are going through a similar situation in your life right now. Or maybe you know someone who is enduring a trying time. In your heart, you really want to reach out to the people you love who have given up hope. Your heart reaches out to them in empathy and sympathy, and yet, the truth of the matter is, sometimes we are at a loss for words and we just don't know what to say. What do you tell a person who is on a long, slow slide into despair?

We learn from Paul that our hope is inextricably connected to our knowledge of who we are as God's chosen, adopted, forgiven, accepted people. Who are we?

- John 1:12 says, "We are the children of God."
- 1 Peter 2:9 says, "We are a peculiar people, a holy nation, a royal priesthood."
- Romans 8:17 says, "We are heirs of God and joint heirs of Jesus Christ."
- 2 Corinthians 5:20 says, "We are ambassadors for Christ."
- Psalm 107:2 says, "We are the redeemed who should say so."
- Matthew 16:18 says, "We are the church that was built on a rock."

We are the servants of the Most High, the Almighty, the Everlasting God. Yes, storms come, winds blow, and lightning flashes, but we don't have to give up because we know who we are and whom we serve. We are the King's children. We are the servants of the Almighty God. Remember this, and you won't lose your mind. You won't go crazy or become depressed. How do we hang on? And how do we help other's hang on? We recognize that we serve a God who's got all power in his hand and a legion of angels to help us get through. No matter how dark things look, we find light in the goodness and greatness of God, we find hope when we remember that his angels are constantly looking out for us, and we find courage as we realize we are children of the King! These strong truths reshape our emotions and transform them (gradually if not quickly) from despair to a strong, vibrant hope in God.

CHAPTER 4

WHEN YOU FEEL LIKE QUITTING, BUT YOU CAN'T

Then I said, "I will not make mention of him,
Nor speak anymore in his name."
But his word was in my heart like a
burning fire
Shut up in my bones;
I was weary of holding it back,
And I could not. —Jeremiah 20:9

In moments of despair, we learn a thing or two about ourselves. Most people realize that completely letting go and totally calling it quits is just not in them. In that nano-second before completely giving up, most people prove they have an innate desire to fight against injustice and overcome heartache. This tenacity is the essence of courage.

Usually, this flame of hope starts small, with only a spark, but it's enough to get started. Every good and proper response in our lives begins with a single step. It doesn't matter if it's running a marathon, overcoming an addiction, applying for a job, restoring a marriage, reconnecting with a child, launching a new product, or writing a book, you can't finish if you don't start. For some of us, starting is the hardest part.

JUST A SPARK

The flame of change doesn't begin as a roaring fire, but eventually, the spark ignites the kindling of hope, and the fire begins to burn hot and bright. In the spiritual world, the initial spark of hope enflames our desire to survive. Then it grows, little by little. Rarely does it go "from zero to sixty in 4.3 seconds." It's more like zero to sixty in days, weeks, or even months. In some cases, the growth is so slow that a person doesn't realize how much progress has happened until she looks back a few days or weeks and can say, "Wow, look how far I've come!"

In those flashes of reflection, we see genuine progress in overcoming the desire to quit. Cancer patients—and everyone who experiences any kind of trauma or the heartache of significant loss—are devastated by the first news of the diagnosis. After the reality sinks in, their thought is, "How can I get over this? What can I do to make this go away?" After a season of anger and bargaining, they begin to genuinely grieve their losses and trust God for whatever may come their way. When actor Patrick Swayze was first diagnosed with cancer in March 2008, he was given just weeks to live. He fought his disease before succumbing to it in September of 2009. He never quit, no matter how bleak it looked.

When have you felt like quitting but realized you can't? No matter how bad things look, even in the face of death, we shouldn't quit on God. We can hang in there with him, trusting that the spark of faith will grow to a bright flame of trusting in him through thick and thin. Sometimes, God rescues us *out of* our trouble, but more often, he rescues us *through* our difficulties. Facing them with a heart of faith isn't escape; it's a faith that honors God and brings a smile to his face.

Many different struggles can cause us to want to give up and quit. It could be quitting a job, quitting an organization, quitting a marriage, quitting a relationship with a friend, quitting school, quitting the choir or some other ministry in the church, or quitting life altogether. The list of headaches and heartaches is almost endless. The desire to escape pain isn't subhuman or inhuman. Even Jesus, the bravest and strongest person who ever lived, wanted to run when he realized the pain he would experience on the cross—but thank God, he didn't quit!

If you've never felt like quitting, then you haven't lived very long—or you're not being honest with yourself about the pain you've experienced. The desire to avoid pain can cripple us emotionally and isolate us relationally. Some of us are afraid to get involved in others' lives because we don't want to take the risk of failure or rejection. Anyone who would dare to step into the arena of leadership, fellowship, or membership where interaction with other people is required sooner or later will come to a moment when he feels like quitting. Difficult circumstances, disagreements, and unfulfilled expectations can tempt us to raise the white flag of surrender and say, "I quit. That's all I can take. I'm out of here!"

NEVER GOOD ENOUGH

Have you ever felt that your life was Mission Impossible? No matter how hard you tried, it was never good enough. You tried to make your marriage better, but it didn't work. In fact, the more you tried, the worse it got. You tried to be a great parent, but your kids resented your efforts to care for them and steer them in the right direction. No matter how hard you tried in your relationships with your children, your efforts failed. That little knuckleheaded boy, or that little hardheaded girl of yours keeps rebelling and keeps pushing you away, and the more you try, the worse it gets. You've tried to manage your money well, but you live under a mountain of debt. You tried hard to be a great employee, a terrific friend, and a good son or daughter to your parents, but every effort has turned to dust. Everywhere you turn, it seems you're facing Mission Impossible.

You can be absolutely certain that you're in the will of God, and you know you're doing what God wants you to do, but the more you try, the worse things get. But God never promises that being in his will protects us from harm. In some ways, following Jesus necessarily leads us into trouble! He said that when we live for him, our faith makes waves. And when we value what he values, we cut against the culture's grain—and against the expectations of people who are watching us. But God has a purpose in our pain. When we face difficulties and we come to our wits' end, we stop depending on ourselves and become desperate for God. That's at least one of his purposes in letting us experience life's difficulties. Sometimes, God lets you get into a situation that you can't fix—you're not smart enough, and you're not strong enough. When you've come to the end of your own abilities and resourcefulness, you look up and say, "Father, I stretch my hand to thee!" That's exactly where he wants us.

When we try to avoid pain at all costs, we miss God's purpose for it. C. S. Lewis said that pain is "God's megaphone to get our attention." In his outstanding book, *Knowing God,* J. I. Packer observed that God has a higher purpose than helping us avoid pain. He wrote,

> "This is what all the work of grace aims at—an even deeper knowledge of God, and an ever closer fellowship with Him. Grace is God drawing us sinners closer and closer to Him. How does God in grace prosecute this purpose? Not by shielding us from assault by the world, the flesh, and the devil, nor by protecting us from burdensome and frustrating circumstances, nor yet by shielding us from troubles created by our own temperament and psychology; but rather by exposing us to all these things, so as to overwhelm us with a sense of our own inadequacy, and to drive us to cling to Him more closely. This is the ultimate reason, from our standpoint, why God fills our lives with troubles and perplexities of one sort or another—it is to ensure that we shall learn to hold Him fast."[3]

JEREMIAH: STAYING STRONG

Pain, though, is seldom a welcome teacher. One of the biggest heartaches we experience is personal rejection.

Jeremiah represented God to the people of Israel, but they rejected his message and him. They tried to ignore him, but when he wouldn't stop speaking God's word to them, they laughed at him. At one point, Jeremiah prayed, "Lord, I'm in derision daily; everyone mocks me" (Jeremiah 20:7). The word *derision* means "to be to laughed at, to make fun of someone." Jeremiah said, "Lord, these people aren't taking me seriously. They're laughing at me. They're making fun of me, Lord. They think I'm a fool. I'm telling them what you told me to tell them. You told me to warn them, and you told me not to sugarcoat it. You told me to tell them to repent and turn from their wicked ways, but they only laughed at me. I'm in derision daily." Can you feel the pain in Jeremiah's words? He had been faithful to God, but the people completely rejected him. In fact, they didn't even pay him the compliment of trying to refute his arguments. They just laughed at him.

Few things are more frustrating than to be taken lightly by people we value, especially when we want to be taken seriously. Every teenager knows this frustration. She needs to talk, sometimes desperately, but she feels brushed aside by a parent who appears too busy doing other things. The teenager turns to friends who will listen—in fact, *anybody* who will listen and take her seriously!

We "blow people off" and try to ignore them if they don't contribute to our welfare and comfort. We blow off family and friends, co-workers and neighbors, sometimes with disastrous results. Quite often, people who are hurting give us warning signs that they need our help, but we don't notice.

Occasionally, deeply disturbed people "go postal" and kill people who didn't pay attention to them. Tragically, the only time institutions pay them any attention is when they mentally snap and murder people. Most of us don't respond to neglect in this extreme measure, but we all suffer when the people we love don't notice our needs. A wife feels disregarded when her husband cares more about sports, work, fishing, a hobby, his friends, or television than her. She wants a serious, loving relationship, but he doesn't seem to care. And a husband longs for his wife to notice how hard he works for her and the kids. Everyone wants attention, affirmation, and affection.

Moments of perceived or actual rejection turn into long seasons of frustration, inevitably leading us to the depths of despair. When heartache in a relationship isn't remedied, disappointment becomes the normal fare of life, and two people drift apart, living at best in an armed truce—nothing like the loving relationship they committed to build at the altar or at the child's birth years before. The pain stretches on without an end in sight.

Jeremiah concluded sadly, "Then I said I would not make mention of [God] nor speak anymore in his name." I can see Jeremiah in my imagination as he slowly gets up from his desk and walks across the room and stares at a wall upon which hangs his prophetic license and his certificate of ordination. He stares at them for several moments, and then all of a sudden, he angrily snatches them off the wall and screams, "You know what? I'm quitting! I'm not going to continue to take this abuse and this disrespect from these rebellious people. I'm going to turn my ordination papers back into God and tell him to get somebody else to do the job—because I quit!" He throws his books away because he has no intention of coming back. He furiously kicks the last vestige of memories of walking with God, and he storms out of the room, slamming the door behind him!

PIVOT POINTS

Have you ever been at the point where Jeremiah was on that day? Have you felt like saying, "I quit, God! Get somebody else to do this job"?

- I know a number of single parents who are doing the best they can to raise their children by themselves. The strains of work and parenting, though, are enormous. Virtually all single parents eventually crack under the stress and feel like saying, "I quit!"
- A married person feels his marriage is over, and there's no way it's going to be saved. There's nothing further to be done. In these situations, he feels like saying, "I quit!"
- A manager trained a sharp new employee, who then was promoted over the long-term manager. The faithful manager has worked tirelessly and was underpaid, and now feels unappreciated. He feels like saying, "I quit!"
- A senior citizen feels her family has deserted her. The family treats her as though she's "in the way." She feels like saying, "I quit!"

- A person struggles for years with a painful, chronic illness. The financial cost and the emotional burden become so heavy that he gives up and concludes, "What's the use? I'm never going to feel any better. I quit!"
- All of us experience times in this life when we face those low moments, which some have called "the dark night of the soul." In these painful, bleak moments, we feel like telling God and the world, "I quit!"

What makes each of us want to quit? There may be many different factors. Sometimes we suffer under a black cloud of colossal past failures, and nothing makes us want to quit more than one more failure. Many psychologists, though, say that the fear of rejection is our deepest, darkest fear. Some us look at our lives and conclude that every relationship we've treasured has fallen apart, and we want to say, "I quit." We reach out to connect with someone, but the person seems to push us away. After a while, even trying to have a relationship seems like too much trouble.

This downward spiral continues until we're completely worn out and fatigue takes over. *Fatigue* describes a range of afflictions, varying from a general condition of tiredness to a burning sensation in over-taxed muscles. It can be both physical and mental. The term, fatigue, doesn't refer to a medical diagnosis. Instead, it is a symptom that is reported by the patient instead of being observed by the doctor. *Physical fatigue* is the inability to continue functioning at the level of a person's normal abilities. It becomes particularly noticeable during rigorous exercise. On the other hand, *mental fatigue* often is seen as drowsiness or the inability to concentrate.

We all know what fatigue looks like and feels like, and we've all experienced it at one time or another. Cramming for a test, caring for infants or elderly people, or trying to finish a big project at work often causes us to become fatigued, both physically and mentally. When we're tired, our margins are thin, and we can't cram one more thing into our busy schedules.

Fatigue can be the result of many different things: putting in long hours at work, unrelieved mental stress, jet lag, intense physical activities, or major depression. It can also be the unwanted product of prolonged boredom, severe physical illness, or a recurring lack of sleep. Also, fatigue can be the consequence of chemicals in the body, such as an addiction to a substance, poisoning, or vitamin and mineral deficiencies. Massive blood loss frequently results in anemia, which causes the body to feel exhausted. Too much stress, however, is the most common culprit that causes fatigue.

When we live too long with unrelieved stress, we take *short cuts* and we become *short tempered.* When we're exhausted and pressured, we try to get by with as little effort as possible, we don't give as much attention to detail, we don't concentrate very well, and we're distracted by all the demands we feel. Consequently, we drop the ball, which, of course, compounds our stress because now we have to clean up the mess, spend our energies dodging blame, and suffer additional guilt and shame for being "so incompetent." Stress often surfaces when we are short tempered with family, friends, and co-workers. It poisons every relationship. When we have no room for error or creativity, our language is full of demands instead of grace, and we create conflict instead of fostering understanding. As our stress level rises, we become even more compulsive about controlling difficult people and situations.

In his book, *Margin: Restoring Emotional, Physical, Financial and Time Reserves to Our Overloaded Lives,* Dr. Richard Swenson observes moderate levels of stress stimulate our creativity and motivate us to accomplish our goals. But stress levels can rise so gradually that we don't notice them. As tension escalates, we experience negative impact of too much pressure, and we fail to notice the problem and make changes. Under severe and unrelieved pressure, we make poor decisions and every part of our lives is adversely affected. We seethe with anger when anyone gets in the way, we experience physical problems such as headaches and stomach problems, our relationships suffer, and our effectiveness declines. At that point, we can experience the devastation of burnout.[4] When this occurs, the light at the end of the proverbial tunnel is a train headed in our direction! Laying down on the tracks to end it all sometimes seems like the best option. Ending it all appears to be a preferable solution than facing the Mt. Everest-sized challenges. They look like a mountain we'll never be able to climb, and we find ourselves at the place where we want to say, "Lord, I quit."

But is that really the answer? Look back at Jeremiah for a moment. The prophet received his call to serve God at an early age, during the thirteenth year of King Josiah's reign over Judah. As a young man, he planted his life in Jerusalem, and for forty years he was the Lord's messenger during the troubled days of the southern kingdom. His message and ministry was to prophesy to a people who were sinful, stubborn and stiff-necked, and who had been misled by false prophets. His God-given task was to be a faithful witness of their impending doom. He saw his nation pass from happy and prosperous times to an era of utter sinfulness and rebellion. However, Jeremiah didn't delight in telling them about God's righteous judgment. It sent him into a deep depression. In fact, he became so depressed that he was known as "the weeping prophet." As he spoke God's condemning message and wept over the people's sins, he became emotionally and physically exhausted. His message failed to turn the people back to God, so a sense of abject failure was added to his exhaustion. He wanted to tell God, "You deceived me. I thought it was going to go another way. You called me, but it looks like my role has been a colossal failure. I quit!"

Although Jeremiah was ready to quit, we can find some good news in his story. He went home that night and made the announcement to his wife, "Honey, I want you to know something. I just quit my job today. I quit the church. I'm not going to preach any more. I'm done with God and his plan for my life. In fact, I'm not even going to mention God's name anymore. I'm through with these people. They're hardheaded, and they won't listen to a thing I have to say. I'm quitting. I'm sure you understand." He may have seen "that look in her eye," so he told her, "Don't try to talk me out of this. I don't want to hear anything from you. Don't give me any lip. I'm telling you, I quit!"

I can picture Jeremiah getting out of the shower, putting on his pajamas and getting into bed. He tries to sleep, but he tosses and turns all night long. And then Jeremiah says, "I began to feel a warm sensation all over my body. And the more I tried to fight it, the hotter I got!" Finally, it got so hot that he sat straight up in his bed and had his hand on his head and said, "Lord, as much as I want to quit, I realize I can't! This calling on my life is more than I can bear. And the more I understand that you're in the middle of it, the more I realize I can't quit. This power behind me is a force that I can't resist." He announces to his surprised wife, "God's word was in my heart like a burning fire, shut up in my bones. I can't quit!"

Jeremiah was an Old Testament prophet, but his life dramatizes a common experience for all of us. He describes the dilemma of every person who has a calling on his or her life—and that's *all of us* who claim to know Jesus Christ as our Savior and Lord. When you come to those moments in life when you want to quit, you discover that as much as you want to quit, your calling, your purpose, your destiny, and your assignment won't let you give up and walk away. We may wrestle with our feelings, our role, and God, but in the end, we realize that we simply have to stand and fight.

We may think we're weak and hopeless, but we're not. Jeremiah wasn't a tough guy. He was sensitive and kind. If he could find the will to fight on, we can, too. What are some of the things you have overcome in your life, and what have you done to overcome them? Earlier I mentioned that a fire starts small and then grows. When you were ready to quit, what was the spark that gave you faith, hope, and courage to keep going? Did God use the power of his Word, the nudge of the Spirit, the encouragement of a friend, or his "still, small voice" to remind you that he has a wonderful plan for your life? How did your confidence grow? What caused your energy to increase and your outlook to change?

Jeremiah's experience teaches us three crucial principles:

- At times, life will be frustrating,
- Low moments may cause us to feel like quitting, and
- The good news is that the Lord will give us what we need to persevere.

The purpose of our lives springs forth from an unquenchable fountain. It comes from God himself. We may drift along in despair for a while, but suddenly, God shows up and gives us the strength we need. The Holy Spirit reminds us, "I'm with you. Don't quit. I'll encourage you. Lift up your hands, and be encouraged. You can trust me, so don't quit." Stay in the race. Never, ever quit. If you stay in the fight, you'll overcome. Sooner or later, you'll win. You'll finish the race, and you'll finish strong. That's the guarantee of Almighty God. Count on it.

CHAPTER 5

A SHELTER IN THE STORM

Be merciful to me, O God, be merciful to me!
For my soul trusts in you;
And in the shadow of your wings I will
make my refuge,
Until these calamities have passed by.
—Psalm 57:1

In the mid-90s, people went in droves to see the movie *Twister*. At one time, the film ranked thirteenth on the all-time list for domestic gross box office receipts. The movie depicts the self-imposed terror of storm chasers in the Midwest. The plot includes a love story and competition between teams who try to outfox and out-drive each other to get into the center of tornadoes. The groups of storm chasers follow twisters in an effort to deploy a new mechanism designed to help scientists understand the dynamic nature of the storms. Many times the characters in the film are forced to flee meandering storms and run for their lives. In order to survive, they have to run fast and find shelter—but not just any shelter will do. It has to be a strong shelter that can shield them from the powerful and destructive ravages of the storm.

THE ILLUSION OF SAFETY

When we experience the storms of life, we need a shelter, too. Those who live in the South have endured their share of thunderstorms and hurricanes. People in the Midwest, like those depicted in the movie, face the threat of devastating tornadoes. Residents in the North worry about blizzards and cold so severe that being caught outside can mean life or death. In the Northwest, volcanoes can erupt at any time and avalanches can wipe out wide swaths of land. And of course, Californians live with a constant nervous twitch because earthquakes are a common occurrence.

There are no safe places in this country. We all need a shelter at one time or another. Perhaps you haven't lived through a tornado, but you no doubt have seen the aftermath of its destructive power in news reports. You've seen how these storms can blow houses off of their foundations, destroy entire communities, snap trees like toothpicks, and scatter debris for miles. The force of tornadoes can be as powerful as a nuclear weapon.

These storms are dangerous and deadly, and we should take them very seriously when they come. Whenever a tornado warning is given, authorities tell us to seek shelter by going to the lowest part of our homes, or perhaps into a central closet, and staying away from the windows. The storms have the power to kill, and our survival depends on us finding the proper shelter.

NOT THE CAVE

After David was anointed as king over Israel, he didn't take the throne immediately. In fact, Saul was still king, and he was fiercely jealous of David's popularity. They young man became a fugitive, running for his life with a price on his head. Saul repeatedly tried to kill him, so David found himself constantly running and hiding. King Saul was deeply insecure and easily threatened. Because of his spiritual bankruptcy, Saul wanted to kill an innocent man.

When David was hiding in a cave in En-gedi, he cried out, "Be merciful to me, O God, be merciful to me! For my soul trusts in you; and in the shadow of your wings I will make my refuge, until these calamities have passed by" (Psalm 57:1). David understood that his shelter was not really the cave. His ultimate shelter was God.

King Saul gathered 3,000 of his choice men to search among the caves where David had hidden. The Bible says that at one point, Saul was in the same cave with David, but he was unaware of David's presence.

David's followers saw the situation as a golden opportunity for David to kill Saul and claim the throne, but David said, "No, I'm not going to touch God's anointed." Instead, David cut off the bottom of Saul's robe, and after the king had walked out into the sunlight, David yelled to him and showed him that he had it in his power to kill him, but he didn't do it. David understood that God would be his shelter, even in a cave with his sworn enemy only a few feet away.

David knew that the storms of life come, often when we least expect them. Though life may be tranquil right now, don't be fooled. Sooner or later, the storm clouds of trouble, distress, and misfortune are going to come. If we're going to survive them, we need to follow David's example and trust that God will be our shelter.

In David's song of trust in Psalm 57, the first thing we are told to do is make our requests known to God. David asks God to show him mercy and rescue him. His request teaches us about how to pray when we need a shelter in the storm. We can be completely honest with God about our needs because he values our relationship with him and will make himself known to us if we'll cry out to him. The prayer in this psalm suggests that David had a *personal* relationship with God. The relationship didn't guarantee an easy life, but it gave David a refuge in times of trouble.

TRYING TO BARGAIN WITH GOD

God prevents many storms, but not all of them. Just because you have a relationship with God doesn't exempt you from facing times of trouble, difficulty, and misfortune. Sometimes, we can try to make deals with God to make our troubles go away. When we're going through a difficult time, we may think, "If I just go to church, and maybe if I sing in the choir and tithe this month, my troubles will vanish."

This may sound strange coming from a pastor, but joining a church, singing in the choir, or giving a check to the church may not be the best solution to a person's problems. God doesn't make deals like this. He has a plan to bless us, but some of his greatest blessings come in the midst of struggles. If we try to escape them, we miss his blessings. In fact, when we live for God, our troubles might increase, not decrease. Rest assured, Satan is going to see to it that you face trouble when you get serious about living for God. The evil one will do everything he can to discourage you so that you'll give up on God.

Though storms come, we won't have to face them alone. God values the relationship he has with us. When storms come, we can follow David's example and run to God to find a shelter. We can run to God in prayer, and we don't have to go to him timidly and scared. Instead, we can come boldly before his throne and make our requests known to him. There, we will find the grace, the mercy, and the help we need to survive—and thrive—in the storm.

SIMPLE PRAYERS OF TRUST

God invites his children, "Call on me in your time of need, and I will answer." Because we have a relationship with God, he invites us to ask, and we shall receive; seek, and we shall find; knock, and the door shall be opened to us. David says when we make our requests known to God, we can be confident that he hears us because God values our relationship with him—we are his dearly beloved children.

When David was in trouble in the cave in En-gedi threatened by King Saul and 3,000 men, he didn't have time to pray a long, elaborate prayer. In the moment, he only had time for a simple, brief prayer: "Lord, have mercy. I've got trouble all around me. Lord, have mercy." One little prayer—just a few words. Too many of us get caught up in long, drawn-out prayers. We ramble, we repeat ourselves, and we spend our energies trying to sound spiritual instead of connecting with the Father who loves us. The truth of the matter is, the principle of KISS: "Keep it simple stupid," works just fine in prayer, too.

The next time we're in trouble, we may only have time to pray, "Lord, have mercy." What does *mercy* mean? It means whatever you need, God's got it. If we have a need for finances, "Lord, have mercy." If we have a family problem, "Lord, have mercy." If it's a wayward child, "Lord, have mercy." If we're sick, "Lord, have mercy." Whatever we need, God's got it.

God responds to sincerity. David didn't try to minimize his need. He was very honest about his predicament. He prayed earnestly and boldly, "Be merciful to me, O God, be merciful to me." Did you notice that David utters a double cry for mercy? That's significant. At that moment, David's emotions came to a crescendo. He was at his wits' end as he cried out to God, "Lord, I need you to help me, and I need you to help me right now!"

This is not the first time David cried out for God's help. In the three previous psalms that lead up to Psalm 57, the first verse of each of them, which are also prayers, David says, "Lord, help me."

- In Psalm 54, he asks, "Save me, O God." In other words, "Lord, please help me!"
- In Psalm 55, he says, "Give in unto my prayer, O God, and hide not yourself from my supplication." In other words, "Lord, help me!"
- In Psalm 56, he pleads, "Be merciful to me, O God, for man would swallow me up." In other words, "Lord, help me!"

Now in Psalm 57, David once again cries out for help. He says, "Be merciful to me, O God. Be merciful to me." His double cry for mercy was an indication of how serious his situation was, but it also demonstrated the sincerity of his heart. David's double cry for mercy tells us that he was at the breaking point, but he hadn't given up on God.

Are you at that point? Behind your smiles, behind your hallelujahs, and behind your hand waving, are you at the breaking point? Are you at the breaking point with a marriage that's falling apart? At the breaking point with your financial situation? At the breaking point with sickness in your body? At the breaking point with your job or your finances? At the breaking point with a prodigal child?

After I'd been at the church in Nebraska for several years, I felt very empty, confused, and without a sense of direction.

I often got in my car to drive around so I could be alone with God. I prayed, "God, it seems that my work here is done. I want to do more for you, but I don't know where to go. Will you lead me?" In the past, I had enjoyed the work God had given me to do, but now I felt I was ineffective. The things I had loved to do—like preaching—became drudgery. I hoped God had something else and something more, but I had no idea what it was. Many leaders say that we often have to experience "the death of a dream" before God resurrects it as something far better than we ever imagined. The dream may be a particular career or a cherished relationship. We pray, we work hard, but inexplicably, it all turns to dust. If we hang in there with God, however, he creates something beautiful out of the rubble. That's what happened to me. After months of wrestling with God, I sensed he was leading me to a smaller church in a smaller city. It didn't seem to make sense, but his call was clear, so I chose to obey. I prayed, "Lord, I owe you everything, and you owe me nothing, but if I take this role, will you promise to bless me? Will you pour out your resources on our church and bless us beyond measure?" And he did. In the first four years in Macon, four thousand people joined our church! We've had to build new facilities in two locations to accommodate all the people who come. I've seen the death and the resurrection of a dream, and it's wonderful.

Every now and then, we come to moments of breaking points, and we have "a Popeye moment." The beloved cartoon character from our youth sometimes got so frustrated with life that said, "That's all I can stand, and I can't stand no more!" The point of desperation is the moment when we give up on our self-effort and finally turn to God. He may have been waiting for us to come to this point for a long, long time, and he responds to our cry of desperation like a loving mother responds to her child's cry for help.

God hears our cry of sincerity. You don't have to worry about the eloquence of your prayer. If you mean it from your heart, it doesn't have to be cute, clever, long, or full of intricate theology. It just has to be an expression of your heart's desire. If all you can say is, "Lord, have mercy," say it with honesty and passion. God wants us to come to him without pretense or pomp. He longs for his children to be authentic with him.

When storms threaten to destroy us, we can make our requests known to God. And when we need a shelter in a storm, we can depend on the refuge of God. How is God a refuge for us? First, God himself is our refuge—not his deliverance or his provision, but God himself. David says, "Be merciful to me, O God." The word *God* in this passage is *Elohim.* It is one of the ancient names of God, and it means "the Almighty Maker and Creator of the Universe." David says, "When I need a shelter in the time of my storm, I run to *Elohim.* I go to the Maker, the Creator, whose power and might are unlimited! I can trust him because nothing is too difficult for him!"

David is implying, "God, since you made the world and everything there is, surely you can handle what I'm facing right now. If you were able to make the sun and put it in the sky, surely you can handle my problems. If you could hang 'the celestial chandeliers'—the billions of stars of the universe—I can trust you with my circumstances. If you could carpet the earth with the green grass, nail it down with the daffodils and lilies, and make the fish and put them in the sea, surely you can handle King Saul and his men who have surrounded me."

The God who used his power to create the world is the One that can handle your wayward child, those financial problems, the career difficulties, and the disease that threatens your body.

David says, "God, my soul trusts in you." The word *trust* means "to find refuge in, to hope in, to run to for safety." He says, "God, I know where my refuge lies. It's in you. My help is not in my intelligence or my wit, it's not in my bank account, and it's not in my contact list on my Blackberry. My help is in the name of the Lord." I can have all the money in the world, but money can't solve every problem. People on my Blackberry contact list can't get me out of some problems, and certainly, they can't save me from sin and hell. My IQ and my skills don't really matter, but my help is in the name of the Lord. The psalmist wrote, "I will lift up my eyes to the hills—from whence comes my help? My help comes from the Lord who made heaven and earth" (Psalm 121:1-2)

If you are in a storm, your refuge is in the person of God.

David reflects on God's care: "And in the shadow of your wings, I will make my refuge." When the Bible talks about wings in relation to God, it's a metaphor for God's protective powers. We get a picture of a mother hen who calls her chickens unto herself and spreads her wings to protect them from hawks or other dangers. When she sees a predator about to attack her chicks, she calls them to find shelter under her wings where they find safety and protection. To get to the vulnerable chicks, the hawk or fox has to come through the hen. I don't know about you, but I don't want to mess with mamma!

David uses that picturesque language to describe his dependence on the protection of God. He said, "God, when my trouble comes, I know where I need to run. I need to hide under your wings. The only way the schemes of the enemy are going to get to me is to first get through you—and that's not going to happen!"

I am under no illusions about my competence to protect myself. The reason the enemy hasn't wiped me out isn't because I'm so smart, handsome, clever, or connected with "the right people." It was because God was hiding me and sheltering me.

When you're in trouble, you can tell God, "Hide me, Lord. Hide me from the lies of my enemies. Hide me, Lord. Hide me from the attacks of those who don't like me. Hide me, Lord. Hide me from those who want to harm me. Hide me, Lord." And sometimes you need to tell God, "Hide me from myself, Lord. Hide me from making a dumb mistake." We need God because he can handle our problems infinitely better than we can handle them.

David uses the word *calamities* in this verse to describe the difficulty of his predicament. The word means "trouble, evil, misfortune, or disaster." David said, "God, this is a matter of life and death! I'm facing the potential of destruction and disaster. Help me, Lord!" Years ago, I saw the National Geographic Channel television series Seconds From Disaster. The program investigated man-made and natural disasters. Each episode depicted a single incident by analyzing the causes and circumstances that ultimately affected the disaster, from train wrecks to earthquakes.

When David was in the cave surrounded by Saul and his men, he was only seconds from disaster. He says, "God, I don't have time to pray a long prayer because Saul's got 3,000 men looking for me. And here he is, in the same cave with me! God, I'm seconds from disaster. But as bad as it looks, I realize you can handle it."

You need God because you can't handle the difficulty of your problem on your own. You need him because he can handle it—in fact, he can handle absolutely anything. God knows how long to let you stay in the fire. Don't worry. It may get hot, but God won't let you burn. He knows when to get you out. That's why you need him, because he's in control of the duration of your problems.

Finally, you need God because he can deliver you from your problem. Last thing David says, "In the shadow of your wings I will make my refuge, until these calamities pass by." When we analyze storms, we realize they all have one thing in common, whether it's big storms or little storms—they eventually pass by. You may have been in the storm a long time, but the storm will eventually pass over. The old folks say, "I'm so glad that trouble don't last always."

I'm not going to wait until my trouble leaves before I give God praise. Since we know difficulties will pass, we should praise him while we're in a shelter *during* the storm.

When I was a boy, I used to watch westerns at the theater. I noticed that the cowboys always hid behind the wagons when they were attacked. When one of them got ready to make his move, he would say to his partners, "Cover me!" That's what I tell God every morning before I leave the house. "Lord, cover me. Cover my wife, and cover my children. Cover me when I'm on the airplane. Cover me when enemies are all around me. Cover me when I'm confused about the direction you want me to go. Cover me when people are lying about me. Cover me from the storms today. Thank you, Lord, for your care."

God has given us a number of images to help us understand how he protects and provides for us in times of trouble. He's the shelter from the storm, a hen who protects us from predators, and a covering posse. We can trust him in any storm. What kind of protection do you need from him today?

CHAPTER 6

AN INVITATION TO REST

For my yoke is easy and my burden is light.

—Matthew 11:30

At intervals along the Interstate Highway System, we pass exit signs that read "Rest Areas." These stops are strategically placed along the freeway to allow people to stop and refresh themselves before they continue their journey. The Department of Transportation understands that, in the interest of public safety, they need to provide the public with rest areas. Fighting sleep on a long drive is torture, and it's incredibly dangerous. Have you ever tried to stay awake while you're driving on a long trip? You'll do anything to stay awake! You roll down the windows, turn up the air conditioner, sing to yourself, slap your face, and hang your head out the window like a dog to catch the breeze.

Many years ago, I traveled back home with a friend from a convention in Detroit to Little Rock, Arkansas, where I lived at the time. Early that morning, I got behind the wheel and started to drive. We had about ten hours ahead of us, but my pastor friend wasn't good company. He didn't want to talk, and after a few hours, I was terribly bored, tired and sleepy. I tried to concentrate, but soon I began nodding off. A few times, I weaved and crossed the line dividing the lanes. I was doing my best, but my friend was no help. He was on floor with his head on the seat—sound asleep.

With four hours to go, I didn't think we were going to make it. My head was wobbling like a bobble-head doll on a bumpy road! After going a long way like this, a car behind me flashed his bright lights, so I pulled over. It was a couple of pastors from the conference. When the driver got out, I could tell he didn't want to have prayer meeting. He barked, "Listen, with the way you're driving, you're going to get killed! And maybe some other people on the road too! I know you're sleepy. Why don't you get out, get in the back seat and go to sleep. I'll drive you the rest of the way home." We made it home because we exchanged drivers. I couldn't make it on my own, so I had to let somebody else drive.

THE CURE FOR EXHAUSTION

It's possible not only to be physically tired, but many people today are also emotionally, mentally, and spiritually tired. If this diagnosis describes your current condition, you need some rest.

When we come to those moments in life when we're exhausted, Jesus says, "Pull over. Let me under the steering wheel of your life, and you get in the passenger's seat. I want to give you what you need to make it to your destination."

Jesus said it this way in Matthew 11: "Come to me, all you who labor and are heavy laden, and I will give you rest." Jesus is offering to give us rest. In fact, he's offering to give us what no one else can give us. We can lay our burdens on him because he's a burden-bearer; he's a heavy load sharer. He invites us by saying, "Come to me, because I'll carry your burden."

Jesus' invitation, "Come to me," is in the imperative mood. It's not a suggestion; it's *a command* to direct us and *an invitation* to draw us near. When he says, "Come to me," he is literally saying, "I am the fulfillment of what the writer meant in Psalm 46: 'The Lord is our refuge and strength, a very present help in trouble.'" Jesus is telling us to come to God because he is our source of strength.

Furthermore, following the imperative "Come to me," are the words "all you who labor." The word *labor* means "to grow weary, to grow tired, to be exhausted." It means to be exhausted to the point that you feel like you can't go any further. Jesus is talking to the Jewish people who carried the heavy burden of trying to keep the letter of the Law. The religious leaders had placed an oppressive burden of on the people. They not only demanded that the people observe and follow the ceremonial and moral codes of the Old Testament, but they also added hundreds of new laws and regulations to the list! The burden of keeping all these rules was crushing emotionally and spiritually, and it caused many to give up on God. These leaders made religion drudgery.

Instead, Jesus told people, "Listen, I want to be a leader and shepherd who is not going to issue a long list of heavy rules and regulations that make you weary and feel like giving up." He says, "So come to me, those of you who are tired, who are weary, who are about to throw in the towel. I'll lift the burden and give you true rest." That must have shaken their shackles a bit!

In 1982, Air Florida Flight 90 crashed shortly after takeoff into a bridge over the Potomac River in Washington, D.C. Before the flight, the captain declined to de-ice the aircraft after waiting on the runway for nearly an hour, and a fatal layer of ice built up on the wings. The plane was simply too heavy to fly. Only four passengers and a flight attendant survived. One of those passengers was a woman who nearly died during the rescue effort. She held on to a life preserver as it was pulled across the freezing river, but in the frigid water, she quickly grew tired and gave up. She was slipping under the water when a pedestrian saw her predicament. He immediately stripped off part of his clothing, jumped into the water, swam out, grabbed her, and brought her to shore.

She would have died because she was weary, tired, and exhausted. We get like that in our daily lives. Sometimes we just need to take a break from the intense demands on us. All of us endure heavy burdens at work and at home, but housewives and single moms endure unending loads of caring for others, often with little appreciation or relief. They do everything they can to keep the house going, but they're tired of the cooking, the cleaning, and everything else that goes along with it. They're exhausted from picking up after grown children who won't pick up after themselves, tired of hearing their name called all day long, "Mommy, mommy, mommy!" Without relief and encouragement, they become exhausted and feel like giving up.

Jesus not only invites those who are weary to come to him, he also invites those who are weighed down. He says, "Come to me, all you who labor *and are heavy laden*." The term *heavy laden* means "burdened down, loaded under a burden that's so heavy that it causes your back to bend."

Perhaps you recall driving down the freeway and seeing semi-trailers going by with heavy cargo loaded on the flatbeds. Sometimes the load is so heavy you can see the bed bending down under the weight. Sometimes people are weighed down with religiosity. Like the Pharisees who multiplied rules to prove they were more spiritual than others, some of us do the right things but for the wrong reasons. We are like the elder brother in Jesus' story of two sons. They younger brother squandered his inheritance on wine, women, and song, but the older brother stayed home. He worked hard in his father's fields, but we get a glimpse of his hardened heart when his wayward brother returned. The older son refused to come to the party his father had thrown to celebrate. When his dad came out to beg him to join the feast, the elder brother snarled, "Lo, these many years I have been serving you; I never transgressed your commandment at any time; and yet you never gave me a young goat, that I might make merry with my friends. But as soon as this son of yours came, who has devoured your livelihood with harlots, you killed the fatted calf for him" (Luke 15:29-30). When our hearts are full of self-righteousness like this elder brother, we become bitter and demanding, even though we're in church, serving in various ways, and singing the hymns each week. If our hearts aren't filled with God's grace, we can go through the motions of caring for others, serving, and giving, but these activities feel like burdens instead of ways to show God how much we delight in him. They are duty without beauty. Until we recognize this poison of the soul, we continue to do the right things in order to gain leverage over God so that "he owes us." That's what it means to be "religiously weighed down"—obeying God's rules, but with a heart that's far from him.

I started preaching when I was 16 years old. I was totally dedicated to God, but I didn't have any mentors to help me find a sense of balance. I naively said "no" to a lot of fun things that I could have enjoyed. That year, a nice young lady in my class invited me to take her to the prom, but I thought it was "too worldly," so I turned her down. I wanted to be a good example to the other students in our school, and I sure didn't want anybody to think I had "sold out to the world." I didn't realize that I could have been a far better example if they could have seen me having a good time while I was walking with God. The uptight religious leaders criticized Jesus for going to Matthew's party and hanging out with normal people. It took me a while to understand that "being like Jesus" involves loving people enough to value relationships with them over keeping arbitrary rules. Rigidly following rules robs us of some pleasures God wants us to enjoy, creates distance in relationships, and makes us feel superior instead of humble.

Maybe you're not "religiously weighted," but "domestically weighted." You're in a marriage that causes you misery. You feel rejected and misunderstood, and you hate to go home. Or you may be "financially weighted down," living under a mountain of debt and a cloud of doubt. An uncertain financial future puts a lot of weight on a person. Before you snap, and before you give up, Jesus says, "Come to me. Quit trying to handle it your way. Let me drive. Let me fix it. Let me handle it, and find refreshment for your soul." Jesus assures us, "And I will give you rest."

SPIRITUAL GATORADE

Ahh rest. Can you picture it? Your feet are propped up. Someone is bringing your favorite beverage. You might have the television on, or you might be on the porch with a cool breeze lightly caressing your skin. The word *rest* means "refreshment and replenishment." In 1965, the Florida Gators football team was not playing up to their potential. They were out in the hot, relentless Florida sun, which drained their energy. The coaches noticed the players' lethargy, so the staff asked scientists on campus to come up with a drink that would quickly replenish the players' strength. A short time later, the scientists came up with a new drink. They named it Gatorade. The coaches and players loved it. Gatorade puts back into athletes what the elements sap out of them. Jesus is our spiritual Gatorade. He wants to put back into us what life has zapped out of us. He wants to put back our joy, our enthusiasm, our strength, and everything that facing difficulties has drained out of our lives.

There are two guarantees that come with this refreshment: It's divine and it's free. When Jesus said, "Come to me, all you who labor and are heavy laden," He also added, "and *I* will give you rest." He's saying, "I alone will give you rest. Come to me, because I will give you what nothing and no one else can give you. I alone will give you rest." Some of us are weary, and we're searching for satisfaction and contentment in the wrong places. Some people are looking for rest in drugs. They feel "If I can just get high enough, I will rise above my problems," only to discover that whatever goes up, has to come back down. Others look for rest in the bottle. They figure "If I can just get drunk enough I can pickle my brain and anesthetize my mind to the point that I can escape my problems in my drunken stupor." Guess what happens when the high wears off? The problem is still right there.

We can use virtually any substance, behavior, or relationship as a substitute for God and his rest. We can use work, sports, kids, a career, a hobby, church, or anything else, but they all fail to fill the hole in our hearts. In my childhood church we used to sing, "Can't nobody do me like Jesus, can't nobody love me like Jesus, can't nobody hold me like Jesus. Can't nobody do me like Jesus. It's in Jesus; it's in Jesus." You can't get this from Buddha, Krishna, or Mohammed. Jesus, and only Jesus, can give you replenishment.

And notice He says, "I will give you…." *Give* means it's free. He doesn't say, "I will sell you…." He gives his grace and strength to us as a benefit of our relationship with him.

When was the last time you asked the Lord to refresh you? When did he replenish you? Have you ever gone to church with a negative, sour attitude and left the church with a thankful heart? Have you come to church tired, but by the time you got through hearing the choir sing you found yourself refreshed? Have you ever gone to church sad with your head down, but when the sermon was preached you wanted to praise God?

AN EASY YOKE

We're refreshed and replenished when we allow Jesus to take our yoke. His direction, "Take my yoke," implies he's going to give us something if we give him something. A yoke was an instrument of animal husbandry, a piece of wood carved by the craftsman to fit over the neck and shoulders of an ox, on which a burden would be attached. If the yoke was too tight on the ox's neck, it cut into the animal's neck when the burden was placed upon it, making the burden hard to carry. But if the yoke fit well, if it was carved out right and it fit comfortably on the ox's neck, it made the burden easier to carry.

Legend has it that Jesus was a master yoke-builder because he was the son of a carpenter. I don't know if that's true, but if it is, maybe Jesus was drawing from his childhood experiences when he worked in the shop with his daddy, making the yokes for the oxen's necks.

In his stories, Jesus often used items familiar to people to tell stories and make points. In this case, he is saying, "I want you to come to me. And I want you to trade in your tight, heavy, uncomfortable yoke for my yoke, because my yoke is easy." In other words, his yoke fits well. The yoke he puts on you will enable you to effectively carry the burdens of life.

As I mentioned earlier in this chapter, the Jewish leadership had put on the people a massive, heavy yoke that didn't fit well. They added oppressive laws, rules, and regulations that made a sin of just about everything they did on the Sabbath day. The people were discouraged because they couldn't live up to all these additional rules.

Some of us are defeated because we're trying to hold on to things when we need to give them to Jesus. He says, "Cast all your cares upon me because I care for you." If we're going to get relief, we've got to have a fair trade. In giving him our cares and fears, he's asking us to get into the Word. He wants our faith to be an informed faith so that when we come to church and shout, we don't shout in ignorance, but in truth and grace. The enemy, however, defeats some of us because our faith is not well informed. We haven't gotten into the Word. We don't go to Bible study, we don't go to Sunday school, and we seldom pick up the Bible and read it for ourselves. And we wonder why we keep losing spiritual battles! Biblical insight is a source of life to everything we do. Theologian and scholar Thomas Merton observed, "By reading the scriptures I am so renewed that all nature seems renewed around me and with me. The sky seems to be a pure, a cooler blue, the trees a deeper green. The whole world is charged with the glory of God and I feel fire and music under my feet."

You've got to go to boot camp to get ready for battle. If you don't know how to fight, you're going to lose. You need some faith training. When you go to Sunday school, read your Bible and apply what you learn. When you attend a Bible study, you're receiving extra doses of the Word you'll need to face the arrows of doubt and temptation the enemy shoots at you. Make no mistake: It's a fight out here. Every day we've got to fight just to live holy lives. We've got to fight to do right when everybody else is doing wrong. You've got to get the Word into you if you're going to have some relief from the world's deceptions.

Jesus invites us, "Take my yoke upon you and learn from me, for I am gentle and lowly in heart." And then he promises, "For you will find rest for your souls." The second use of the word *rest* in this passage is different than the first one. Here, the word *rest* is a different Greek word that means "to dwell at ease, to relax, to listen, to take the tension off, or to take the tension out." For example, you can tighten the strings on a guitar, but if you tighten them too much, they might snap, and they certainly won't be in tune when you want to play.

In this passage, Jesus is talking to somebody who is about to snap, somebody who is close to going off. Before you lose your mind, go to him because he can give you rest. Some of us live with too much tension. We have tension on the job, then go home and endure tension there, too. If we live in constant tension, we can never relax, replenish, and be refreshed. Without some true spiritual rest, we're not able to live at the level that God wants us to live. Author and pastor Charles Swindoll noted, "Renewal and restoration are not luxuries. They are essentials. Being alone and resting for a while is not selfish. It is Christ-like. Taking your day off each week or rewarding yourself with a relaxing, refreshing vacation is not carnal. It's spiritual. There is absolutely nothing enviable or spiritual about a coronary or a nervous breakdown, nor is an ultra-busy schedule necessarily the mark of a productive life."[5]

I don't know about you, but I don't want to live under constant tension. I want to live burden-free while I rest in him. Is that something you want too? If it is, tell him about it right now. He's listening.

CHAPTER 7

TAKE THE LOAD OFF

Casting all your care upon him, for he cares for you. —1 Peter 5:7

You may be familiar with certain forms of speech called *colloquialisms.* A colloquialism is a particular use of language, a "twist of a phrase" that's sometimes used in informal conversations. Several years ago when I was the pastor of a church in Omaha, my wife engaged in a casual conversation with a man in the church. Our older daughter, Marcie, was about four years old at the time. For security, she often clung to my wife's leg, and during this conversation, she was stuck like glue! The man saw that Marcie felt uncomfortable. To make her feel included, he tried to engage her in the conversation. He leaned over to her, motioned to her with his finger, and whispered, "Come here, and let me put a bug in your ear."

My wife immediately could see the terror on Marcie's face. In her mind, she thought the man was literally going to put a bug in her ear! She started crying because she was too young to recognize the words were just a figure of speech, a colloquialism.

In the South where I pastor a church, we often hear people answer a knock on their front doors by saying warmly, "Come on in! Sit down and take the load off." *Take the load off* isn't about moving pallets of freight with a forklift. The term is about people, and it means "to be at rest, to be comfortable, to have a seat, to transfer the weight of your body off of your feet and onto a chair." Technically, it means you no longer have to carry the weight of your body, but instead you transfer that weight to the seat of the chair. The term, though, has implications in our spiritual and emotional world, too.

In the Bible, the language that communicates *taking a load off* is "casting all your care upon him," which is the secret for us to live burden-free and without anxiety. When Peter wrote his letters to the churches, the Roman government was doing everything it could to stamp out a new faith called Christianity. Believers faced unprecedented persecutions, but in the midst of all the opposition—the anxiety, burdens, and cares of their everyday lives—Peter offers this word of encouragement, "Casting all your care upon him *for he cares for you*" (1 Peter 5:7).

Three things are important to note in this scripture, and they fall under these categories: cares, choices, and competence.

CASTING OUR CARES

In this passage, *care* means "to worry, to be anxious, or to carry the weight of excessive burdens." In his letter, Peter assumes that people undergoing significant persecution are weighed down by the burdens of life—it's a given. To the people who are persecuted and fleeing for their lives, he doesn't ask, "Do you have any cares?" That would be an absurd question. He doesn't say, "Are you feeling like you're weighed down under the burden and the weight of life?" No, he makes the astute assumption that burdens are a present and constant reality in their lives. It's like he's putting his arm around them to say, "I know what you're facing. I know the unprecedented suffering you're enduring at the hands of the Roman government. I know that you have cares. I know you're worried and stressed out, and you're weighed down under the burden of what you're facing today."

In Peter's world and in ours, the conclusion is unmistakable: We have cares. I have cares. You have cares. All of God's children have cares—burdens that cause us to worry, and stresses that cause us to be full of anxiety. Some people arrogantly want you think that nothing ever gets to them. They want everyone to think that they always have it together. They want you to believe they are Superman or Superwoman.

Let's be real about this. There are no Clark Kents running around ready to jump into a phone booth to turn into Superman. We all have secrets, but not the secret of invincibility! We try to hide our vulnerability, but it doesn't work. Everyone knows we're always flawed and often fooled. We carry the weight of the world on our shoulders. It doesn't matter what is the level of maturity of our walks with God, our financial status, age, social standing, or health condition. The plain fact is: We all have cares.

In the Greek, *care* means "to be distracted or be torn in two different directions." It is the metaphorical picture of a garment that is ripped apart at the seams, torn in two different directions. When we're distracted and when we worry, we unravel at the seams of our minds. We are torn between faith and doubt, between hope and fear, and between believing God is sovereign and good and believing that we're on our own.

Peter was aware of the obstacles and the attacks these Christians were up against—the most powerful military might in the world, the Roman government. Believers were people with no military power of their own and no political recourse. The heavy hand of Rome was coming down upon them. Peter also knew there was no light in the immediate future for them. In fact, it was going to get worse.

It's bad enough when you have cares, but isn't it worse when you don't sense any light in the immediate future? When we look around at our world today—at the economy, the environment, the social strife, and the painful, entrenched situations in our daily lives—it doesn't look good, does it? It's enough to depress us, to make us think there's no hope at all. When we lose hope, we quit trying and stop trusting. We get stuck in a hopeless mire of resentment and self-pity. We may face any number of different and seemingly hopeless situations: the mortgage company informs you they want the house back, you're laid off and facing an uncertain financial future, your marriage is strained to the breaking point, or maybe worse, your spouse doesn't pay attention anymore, a child can't stand you or is running with the wrong crowd, a parent is making demands you can't meet, or a friend betrays you. It's enough to depress you, and it's enough to depress me, too! A dark cloud of cares can distract us and depress us.

Depression is one of the most common diagnoses today, but did you know there are millions of people walking around among us in an undiagnosed state of depression? For them, the problem may not be totally debilitating, but these people struggle through life each day with little energy and precious little hope and joy. The things that used to bring pleasure now bore them. They eat too much or too little, sleep too much or not enough, and drift from day to day without any sense of purpose. They don't look for solutions because they've concluded that this is the way life will always be, so what's the use? Cares can stimulate us to trust God and creatively find solutions, or they can crush our spirits.

In addition to emotional and psychological depression, many people suffer from physiological symptoms of stress, including various sicknesses, diseases, and disorders, which are the direct results of worry, stress, and the cares of life. Some people are suffering from heart trouble, others are suffering from ulcers, and some from nervous disorders—all because they worry too much. Some physicians estimate that 70% of patients come to their offices because they experience physical effects of stress in their lives. The symptoms of these patients show up physically at their weakest points. Some experience chronic headaches, some have gastro-intestinal problems, and others suffer from muscle aches and pains. To numb the pain and mask the hopelessness, some people turn to drugs, and not just illegal drugs. Today, there is an epidemic of the abuse of prescription and over-the-counter drugs.

Worry is not just an adult phenomenon. We begin the pattern early in our lives. At the age four in a dark room, we worry about ghosts or vampires (or maybe a sneaky brother). At thirteen, we worry whether or not we'll fit in with the cool group at school. As young adults, we worry about getting stuck in a dead end job, and we wonder if we'll ever get married (or if we've married the right person). As parents we worry about our children. The young executive worries about the presentation that can affect his or her future. The senior citizen worries about possible cuts in Social Security and Medicare. I'm convinced there are many hospital beds, psychiatric wards, drugstores, operating tables, and graves that are signposts of our inability to carry our burdens. We need to find a better way to cope with our struggles.

THE CHOICE: TO CAST OR NOT TO CAST

Many people don't realize they have a choice about what to do with the burdens they carry. There are, in fact, a number of choices each of us can make. One choice is essential: We can give them to God. Peter encouraged us to "cast all our cares upon him." *Casting* means "to place upon, to toss, to get rid, to give it to God." It is the same word that is used by Mark when he wrote, "Then they brought the colt to Jesus and threw their clothes on it, and he sat on it" (Mark 11:7). Peter is saying we can take all of our cares and put them on God, toss them to God, and let him carry them.

Many of us worry about things we can't control, and we neglect to take initiative about the things we can control. Many years ago, pastor and theologian Reinhold Niebuhr wrote what is called "The Serenity Prayer": "God grant me the serenity to accept the things I cannot change; courage to change the things I can; and wisdom to know the difference." That's a wise prayer for all of us—every day. We need God's wisdom and guidance to handle all our cares, including those that are far beyond our control.

Have you ever thrown something in the trash, and later, you went back to retrieve what you threw away? Why did you go back through the trash? Because you weren't through with it. There comes a point in your life where you've got to decide, "I'm through with this worry. I'm not going to be stressed with this problem any longer. I refuse to worry about this difficulty. I can't do anything to change it anyway, so I'm going to give it to God, once and for all."

Notice in Peter's letter that the word *casting* is in the active voice. (Don't be alarmed. This isn't that deep; in fact, it's just eighth-grade grammar.) Active voice means that the subject of the sentence is doing the acting. When the subject is being acted upon, that's passive voice. In this verse about "casting all our cares on Christ," it's active voice. There is no stated subject, but when there's not a stated subject, there's the understood subject: "*You* cast all your care on him"—which means no one else can do it for you. You have to decide to cast *all* your care on God.

Notice *how many* of our cares we give to God. He didn't say, "*Some* of our cares" but "all of our cares": big burdens and little burdens, family burdens, financial burdens, health burdens, relationship burdens, the burdens of employment, the burden of a difficult decision you have to make, the burden of a wayward child, or the burden of a crumbling marriage. He says, "Cast *all* of that on God." Stop trying to hold it yourself, and cast it on his broad, loving shoulders. He can handle it far better than you can.

He says you've got to be through with it, but we often treat our cares like a yo-yo. We cast it to God, and then we worry about it, and we try to take it back. At some point, however, you have to say, "Burden, I can't handle you any more. I'm giving you to God. No argument. I'm not taking you back. You're out of here. Period!"

You can't lift an eighteen-wheeler with an ordinary car jack. Why? Because the jack isn't designed to handle many tons of weight. In the same way, there are some weights people are not designed to handle. Because we can't handle them, we need to give them to God. There's no weight too heavy for God, no burden too big, and no care too difficult. Nothing is impossible for him.

At any point, we have a choice: to carry our burdens ourselves or shift them to God and let him carry them. Many years ago, I went to the UPS Customer Service counter in Omaha, Nebraska to pick up a package. Another man came with an over-sized package on his back. It was so heavy, he staggered and stumbled and almost fell.

I ran over to him as he came through the door. I asked quickly, "Sir, can I help you with that?"

And the man looked at me like he was offended, and angrily growled, "No! I can do it myself!"

I answered, "Well, I was just trying to be a neighbor. It looks like you could use a little help."

A lot of us are like that man. God often says to us, "My son, my daughter, can I help you with that?"

"No! I can do it myself!" we bark.

All around us, we see the evidence of men and women, boys and girls, trying to carry weights we aren't designed to carry. Some of these people are sick and in the hospital right now, because they tried to carry their burdens by themselves. Some are strung out on drugs or alcohol because their burdens are so oppressive they feel the need to escape. Many have stopped going to church because they're trying to make life work without God's power and wisdom. Countless relationships are fractured because people have tried to relate to each other without God's help.

Carrying our own burdens is not the answer. We need to humble ourselves and look to God for help. Peter commands us, "Therefore humble yourselves under the mighty hand of God, that he may exalt you in due time" (1 Peter 5:6).

A few years ago, I saw a brother that I hadn't seen in church in a long time. I was glad to see him, and I asked, "Man, where you been?"

He said, "Pastor, I've been going through so much. I got so many problems in my life, but as soon as I get these problems fixed, I'm coming back to church."

I looked at him long and hard. I then told him, "Brother, you've got it backwards. You ought to be in church even more now. You need God's help to tackle your problems."

He didn't want to hear that. He wanted to fix his problems by himself and then come back to church.

One of the benefits of being a Christian is that we have the Holy Spirit of God inside us. One of the titles for the Holy Spirit is "Comforter." The Greek word for Comforter is *Paraclete,* which means "one who is called along side of us to give us help and aid in our time of need"—that's comfort! The biblical word for comfort, then, isn't just to soothe hurts, but to give us inner strength. The Holy Spirit does more than make you shout and jump when you get happy. The Holy Spirit of God is our Paraclete, the One who comes to aid us, to give us strength and direction in our time of desperate need.

Recently, I was working out at the gym, and I noticed two men lifting very heavy weights on the bench press. These two men were experienced in lifting weights, and they knew that it was dangerous for someone to try to lift alone. In 2009, a young football player at the University of Southern California dropped a bench press bar on his throat, and he suffered severe damage. As I watched the men in the gym that day, one man lifted while the other stood at his head with his hand right under the bar, ready to catch it if the man faltered in any way. He was the spotter. Without a word, he communicated clearly to the other man, "You can do it, and if it gets too heavy for you, I've got you. Don't worry. I've got you."

In the same way, the Holy Spirit is our spotter, and he's trying to tell us, "I've got you. I can help you if you'll let me."

But sadly, some of us wave him off: "I don't need you. I can do it myself!" When we refuse to let the Holy Spirit help us, we're left to our own resources. We might make it for a while, but we're putting ourselves and everyone we love at risk. It's a dangerous choice.

CHRIST'S COMPETENCE

When we refuse the help of the Spirit, we're saying, "I trust me more than I trust you. I believe I'm more competent than you, and I know how to run my life better than you do." How absurd! Christ has proven his power and love through the marvel of creation and the wonder of the cross. We don't have to doubt if he's up to the task to handle our problems! And he's not "out there somewhere" doing his thing, disinterested or uninformed about what's going on in our lives. We can be confident that he will lead us and strengthen us in our time of need. Why? Because, he—cares—for—you!

Let's rephrase that statement to read, "*You* are his concern." He's concerned about you—deeply concerned about you personally. With seven billion other people on the face of the earth, you are still his constant concern. He's in charge of the universe, keeping galaxies and stars from running into one another, but you and I are his concern every moment of every day. We can go to bed at night and get a good night's sleep because we don't need to worry about what we're facing. He knows all about our problems, he's strong enough to work miracles, and he loves us enough to get involved in our lives. We can depend on the One who is Almighty and all loving. Jesus said, "Not a sparrow falls to the ground that your heavenly Father is not aware of." He knows you so well that he knows the number of the strands of hair on your head—or how many used to be there!

When I was a boy, we used to sing a song that says, "When the world seems cold, and your friends are few, there is someone who cares for you, someone who cares, someone who will share all of your burdens like no other can do. You are his concern."

Have you been worried that God can't handle your problems? Don't worry any longer. He can handle them. Peter wouldn't have told us to give our cares to a God who was incompetent or uncaring. That's great news, and it's the secret of burden-free living—that no matter what we face, God can handle it.

- That wayward child of yours—God can handle it.
- Those bills that haven't been paid—God can handle it.
- The mortgage company that's asking for their house back—God can handle it.
- The tough decision you have to make—God can handle it.
- The trials you're facing—God can handle it.

Your problem may be too hard for you, but it's just right for God. Give it to him. Give those burdens, trials, and hard decisions to the Lord. He cares, and he's strong and wise enough to handle them.

Take the load off.

CHAPTER 8

GOD'S BAILOUT PLAN

So she went away and did according to the word of Elijah, and she and he and her household ate for many days. The bin of flour was not used up, nor did the jar of oil run dry, according to the word of the Lord which he spoke by Elijah. —1 Kings 17:15-16

Food prices, fuel and utility costs have been going up. We can bear increased costs if they're small and not very frequent, but if they're too much and too soon, we look at our checkbooks and wonder if we're going to make it. It's more than uncomfortable—it's threatening! It tries our faith. We have to get on our knees to ask God to bless us and sustain us in our time of need.

Sometimes, we need someone to bail us out. How many bailout programs has the government come up with in the last few years? More than you or I care to count. However, unless you're a huge bank or an auto company, you're in the back of the line for a bailout. These are tough economic times for all of us. Not since the Great Depression have we seen such a volatile, fluctuating, and uncertain financial climate. It's so bad our government has had to bail out Wall Street with over $700 billion dollars—all because of out-of-control greed, predatory lending, and inadequate regulation. The world is seeing an economic downturn. In fact, it's the worst economic downturn in almost eighty years. Scores of banks have closed, and many more are in danger of going under. Huge investment firms have been on the brink of collapse. The stock market lost much of its value and is slowly recovering, and a record number of people have lost their homes through foreclosure. Unemployment is a daily disaster for millions of men and women. Today, there are a few glimmers of hope on the horizon, but the near-term outlook is still bleak for many people. The analysts like to remind us that the world financial system teeters on the verge of disaster.

Our government's response to the crisis has been to take our tax money and bail out faltering industries. In addition to the Wall Street bail out, Congress has spent even more on a stimulus package to create jobs. The banks have stabilized, but the jobs haven't materialized. While the government is bailing out Wall Street, many people are wondering who is going to bail out Main Street. Where is the bailout package for people whose company has gone out of business while the greedy Wall Street CEO who drove the company into the ground walks away with a multimillion-dollar golden parachute? It's blatantly unfair, but you and I are footing the bill. We still face daunting challenges—in the Oval Office, in the halls of Congress, and around our family dinner tables.

No matter how well the government handles the crisis, we can be assured that God has a bailout plan of his own. Of course, we still must pay our mortgage to avoid foreclosure, and we still might get laid off from our jobs. We might struggle to pay our bills. However, if we choose to obey and serve God, he has promised to take care of us. No matter how bad it gets, he will make a way for us—if we'll trust him.

We can draw hope from an Old Testament story. In the history of ancient Israel recorded in 1 Kings, a widow was faced with uncertain times like we've recently seen in this country. The story may be ancient, but the application is contemporary. God's bailout plan for this widow is based on three principles: giving, trusting, and God's gracious provision.

GIVING

Giving during tough times may seem counterintuitive, but it's the key to God's storehouse of blessing. Economic conditions may change, but God's requirement that we give has not. God instructs us to give in spite of our circumstances. Yes, times are tough, but he still instructs us to give generously and gladly.

The historian of 1 Kings tells us that the prophet Elijah went to Zarephath to look for an anonymous widow that God told him was going to take care of him. The first woman he saw in the city was this woman. She was gathering some sticks to use as kindling for her stove. She wasn't going to cook just any meal; she was preparing a final meal for herself and her son so they might eat dinner and then wait for death by starvation.

Elijah changed her plans by asking for drink and a morsel of bread. Can you imagine her surprise? The woman stopped and asked, "Don't you realize what I'm going through now. My nation is going through a recession. I've got a hungry mouth to feed. I've got limited resources. My husband is dead. I have only a little grain and a little oil in a jar, and I'm getting ready to use that to fix our final meal before we die. Don't you understand that?"

Elijah understood her situation, but he also understood a bigger truth that God could do the miraculous. He asked her to invite him to dinner, a request that could have sounded incredibly selfish, but it was the doorway to God's blessing in her life. God asked her to give when she had practically nothing. That doesn't make sense to us. Why would God ask this woman to give some of her last morsels of food to a complete stranger?

More importantly, why is God asking you and me to give of our resources at a time of need like our current financial crisis? At a time when unemployment is the highest it has been since the early 1980s, when our banks are going under, and in global economic uncertainty, why is God asking us to give? For one reason: because he wants to show us that our impoverished condition doesn't limit his ability to take care of us. He wants us to give because our breakthrough, our blessing, and our bailout, is determined by our willingness to obey him, not by our bank balance.

The law of sowing and reaping says: In spite of the recession, if you want a harvest, you've got to get some seed in the ground. God wants us to make him our top priority and trust him completely. After the poor widow stated her objections to the prophet's request to share her last meal, Elijah might have said, "What a surprise! I didn't know you were going through all of this. It's all right for you not to give." Instead, he said to her, "Since you only have a meager amount of food for a last meal, fix mine first." In other words, put God first. Make God your priority, and God will show you what he can do for you.

Through the prophet Malachi, God tells us, " 'Bring all the tithes into the storehouse, that there may be food in my house, and try me now in this,' says the Lord of hosts, 'If I will not open for you the windows of heaven and pour out for you such blessing, that there will not be room enough to receive it' " (Malachi 3:10). That's his promise.

The key phrase in this instruction about giving is, "that there may be food in my house." The implication is this: If you take care of God's house, he'll take care of your house. Don't treat God like a second-class citizen. Don't take your resources and pay everything and everybody else, and then, if you have something left, grudgingly give a bit of it to God. That's not the way of spiritual life and blessing! God says, "I want you to make me your priority. Before you give to anything else, give to the one who woke you up this morning and started you on your way, the one who put life in you and blew breath in your body." He said, "Put me first."

TRUSTING

Economic conditions may change, but our trust in God can remain unshakable. The age we live in today is a world of uncertainty, in constant flux. People long for stability, but change is happening all around us: in the economy, in our health conditions, our family relationships, and our jobs. While we live in a world of continual shift, but there's one thing that remains constant: the trustworthiness of Almighty God.

In Elijah's conversation with the widow, she makes a dramatic pronouncement after the prophet asks her to prepare his dinner first. She tells him, "As the Lord your God lives." That's a great confession of trust. The woman isn't a Jew who has been steeped in the teaching of God's truth. She is a Gentile, but she knows enough of the character of God to confess that God lives. In the same statement, however, she reveals that she has the wrong focus. She says, "I have only a little meal in the barrel, a little flour, and a little oil in a jar." The problem with the woman is she makes a good confession, "the Lord lives," but she has the wrong focus—on the scarcity of her resources instead of the wealth of God. She is so convinced that she is going to die that she doesn't believe God will provide for her and her son. She is focusing on what she doesn't have, not what God can produce.

We learn an important principle from this scene: Whenever you are dealing with God, it really doesn't matter what you don't have. As long as he lives, whatever you don't have, God's got it!

Quite often, we exhibit the same problem the woman had. We go to church Sunday after Sunday, and we make great confessions about the existence of God. We say that God can do anything, and he can't fail. That's a great confession of trust. But we leave the church, and we live all week focusing more on our problems than on the living God's ability to provide for us. We have become "practical atheists." We don't live like we believe what we just confessed.

God says, "I want to bail you out. However, I'm waiting on you to learn to trust me. You've got to redirect your focus. Stop looking at what you don't have and start looking at the fact that I'm alive and well." He instructs us, "Give gladly and generously—even though it's a difficult day, give anyway." If we'll give even when we don't have the resources, God will move heaven and earth to provide for us, just like he provided for this poor widow.

To maintain trust, however, you've got to reject fear. F-E-A-R stands for False Evidence Appearing Real. In your times of need, the enemy has been giving you plenty of false evidence. He's told you that you're on your own, that God doesn't care, or that he cares but he's not able to do anything about your problems. These are lies from the pit of hell! When we believe these lies, we hoard our money and refuse to give. Then our goal is protecting ourselves, not opening the door to God's abundant blessings. Fear is one of the most powerful tools of manipulation in the world. When we feel threatened, we become timid and withdrawn. We simply can't live a life of bold faith if we keep listening to those voices communicating false evidence about God and the hopelessness of our situations.

What fears have plagued you? Many of us struggle with voices that whisper or shout that we have every reason to be insecure, because we live with the constant threat of being rejected and failing so badly we'll never recover. The enemy loves to attack us with fear, and he uses our own voices to deceive us. We think that the destructive, accusing thoughts in our minds are normal because they sound so familiar, but they are from the enemy.

Elijah tells the widow, "Do not fear." For this woman's trust in God to break through, her faith had to leap over her fears. Her fears were telling her, "The man said, 'Give me a meal, and fix me a cake,' but I'm in the middle of a recession. I've got a hungry mouth to feed. I'm a single parent trying to raise this boy who is hungry, and I've got to keep cooking for him. I only have a little meal, a little flour, and a little oil. And the man wants me to use the last of my resources for him instead. That's crazy!" Her flesh must have told her, "Child, you can't do that. Don't give your last meal away. If you do, you and your boy are not going to live."

But her faith leaped over fear. She said, "You know, it doesn't make sense. I don't understand it, but I believe the man of God."

Paul wrote to Timothy to explain that God "has not given us the spirit of fear, but of power and love and a sound mind" (2 Timothy 1:7). David wrote, "God is my light and my salvation, whom shall I fear? The Lord is the strength of my life, of whom shall I be afraid? When the wicked, even my enemies and my foes, come against me to eat up my flesh, they stumbled and they fall" (Psalm 27:1-2).

Trusting God requires courage. We've got to reject our fears to live fully and boldly as citizens of his kingdom. We are a King's children, and the King says, "Don't live in fear. Trust me. I will provide even if you run out of resources."

Too many of us allow fear to control us. We won't give of our resources because the enemy gives us false evidence appearing real, telling us, "You'd better use your common sense. God gave you five senses, and you'd better use some common sense." But if we listen to God, we'll use some spiritual sense.

Once we put our fears aside, we'll be able to respond in faith. If we say, "God can do anything but fail," we need to act like we believe it. If we say, "God has all power in his hand," we need to act like we're confident he'll use it. If we say, "God is able to make a way," we need to act on his instructions. If we say, "There is nothing impossible for God," we need to act like we're the children of the King of the universe!

GOD'S PROVISION

Economic conditions may change, but God's ability to provide for us never falters. In Elijah's day, God used a famine to prove to the people that Baal, the false God, wasn't in control of the weather, God seemed to say to the people, "If I've got to do something spectacular, if I've got to let something happen out of the ordinary in order to show you that I'm God, I'll do it." And today, his message to us is, "If I've got to let the global financial markets crash to prove to you that I'm God, I'll do it. I'll use whatever it takes to get your attention, surface your need, and cause you to look up and say to me with the songwriter, 'Father, I stretch my hands to thee. No other help I know.' Even though everything else may be out of control, I still have it under control."

God could have chosen to prove himself by causing the famine and drought to go away just by letting it rain. But God didn't take away the drought. Instead, he provided for the widow, her son, and Elijah in the middle of the worst of times. He'll do the same for us. He doesn't always fix the global and national problems. Sometimes, he leaves these problems intact, but he still provides for people who trust him. This way, he proves that he's Lord above all the governments and markets that claim to rule our lives. They don't; he does. It's like God is saying, "I showed the widow that I could care for her and her son in a weather calamity, and I can take care of you in the midst of a recession when the economy has fallen and the stock market has crashed. No matter what, I'm able to take care of you."

The widow may have had secret doubts about Elijah and God's ability to provide, but she took the bold step of faith to make dinner for him—and a miracle happened! As long as Elijah lived there, the meal and oil never ran out. She gave, and God provided.

When the prophet walked through her door that day, she felt that she was limited by her circumstances and limited resources. When she took a step of faith, however, she discovered an important lesson every believer needs to learn: Our condition doesn't hinder God's provision. It doesn't matter if the flour bin or oil jar is almost empty. Every day, because the poor widow gave, she went into the kitchen and God made sure she had enough flour and oil for another day—just enough for the day, just like the manna God provided for the children of Israel in the Exodus—just for that day. Any extra would go to waste. God seldom gives us an overflowing vat of resources. He wants us to trust him every day to provide just enough for that day's needs. It's enough, and it's miraculous.

When you trust, obey, and give, God may not make you a millionaire. But if you'll serve God, he'll make sure you have enough every day for your needs to be met. As bad as things are, tell yourself, "I'm still here. It doesn't look good sometimes, but I'm still here. I haven't starved to death. God has provided."

Jesus said it this way, "When you pray, you ought to say, 'Give us *this day* our daily bread.'" Some of us are so worried about tomorrow's bread that we let today's bread spoil. The

Lord is trying to remind us to take life "one day at a time." Jesus reminds us, "But seek first the kingdom of God and his righteousness, and all these things shall be added to you. Therefore do not worry about tomorrow, for tomorrow will worry about its own things. Sufficient for the day is its own trouble" (Matthew 6:33-34).

If we focus our hearts on our pitiful resources, we'll end up in despair. But if we focus on God's goodness and greatness, we'll find the courage to trust him to provide—even in our darkest moments. When the widow believed and acted on her faith, the oil and the flour didn't run out. She said, "I'm going to trust the Word of God rather than trusting my circumstances." She's a great example for you and me.

That is the same choice you and I have every day of our lives. We can trust our circumstances, or we can trust the Word. Our circumstances can give us false evidence appearing to be real, but the Word will always be true. Our circumstances may tell us that our trouble is going to last forever, but the Word says, "Weeping may endure for the night, but joy will come in the morning." Our circumstances will tell us that our enemies that are going to wipe us out, but the Word says, "No weapon formed against you shall prosper." Our circumstances will tell us that God is not going to answer our prayer, but the Word says, "They that wait on the Lord shall renew their strength. They will mount up with wings like eagles. They will run and not be weary. And they will walk and not faint." Our circumstances may be telling us that we are failures and will never amount to anything, but the Word says, "You are more than a conqueror through Jesus Christ my Lord."

It sounds pretty simple to me: Trust in God's Word.

- The Word is a lamp to my feet.
- The Word is a light to my path.
- The Word will lift up my bowed down head.
- The Word will keep me in perfect peace.
- The Word will keep my mind stayed on Jesus.

God's bailout plan doesn't allow us to remain passive. Like the widow, we have to find the courage to trust God instead of our circumstances, and our faith has to propel us to take a step of obedience. When you find yourself in times of trouble, listen for the Spirit's directions and take action to obey. Obedience is the doorway to God's provision every day.

CHAPTER 9

THE TESTIMONY OF A CONFIDENT SOUL

He restores my soul;

He leads me in the paths of righteousness

For his name's sake.

—Psalm 23:3

All of us know that God has promised peace, but many of us have the wrong idea about the kind of peace God offers. We think that it's like a great vacation when we're free from every hassle and enjoy life to the fullest. The peace Jesus offers, though, isn't the *absence* of problems, but instead, it's confidence and serenity *in the middle of* problems. On the night Jesus was betrayed and faced the greatest suffering the world has ever known, he told his disciples, "Peace I leave with you, my peace I give to you; not as the world gives do I give to you. Let not your heart be troubled, neither let it be afraid" (John 14:27). And in the most familiar poem in the Bible,

King David wrote about the kind of peace God gives,

"He makes me to lie down in green pastures;
He leads me beside the still waters.
Yea, though I walk through the valley of the shadow of death,
I will fear no evil;
For you are with me;
Your rod and your staff, they comfort me.
You prepare a table before me in the presence of my enemies;
You anoint my head with oil;
My cup runs over" (Psalm 23:2, 4-5).

God's comfort and strength give us peace even in the presence of our enemies and in times of trouble. Our fears, though, block the channel of God's peace. What fears are you facing that keep you from being able to lie down in God's green pastures of faith, hope, and love? Is it financial fears? Is it fears with your health? What friction in your home, at school, or at work keeps you from being able to experience God's presence and joy? What pests bug you? What's causing you to be stressed out? And what hunger do you have? What are areas of desperate or nagging need in your life?

In any and all of these areas of difficulty, you need confidence. *Confidence* is defined as "a state of being certain either that a hypothesis or prediction is correct or that a chosen course of action is the best or most effective." Self-confidence is having a measure of confidence in your abilities and insights. This kind of confidence often results in self-fulfilling prophecy—those without it often fail or don't even try because they're sure they can't measure up, and those with it often succeed because they expect success before they even begin.

Many athletes use visualization to boost their confidence. They visualize game situations and their reactions to those situations *before* they occur. Of course, they spend hours practicing plays, which improves muscle memory, but the extra edge of mental memory is important in developing their confidence.

Have you ever watched Peyton Manning lead the Indianapolis Colts during a comeback drive in the fourth quarter? He exudes confidence! He's sure he'll lead his team to a score, and he's shocked if he doesn't.

During his stellar years with the Chicago Bulls, Michael Jordan wanted the ball in crunch time when the game was on the line in the final seconds. Why? Because he was confident of his abilities to get the job done. Although he failed on numerous occasions, he wasn't afraid to take the final shot to win the game.

We can find that kind of confidence in the words of Psalm 23, considered by many the most beloved in the Old Testament. To some, this psalm may seem old and out-dated, but to many others the six verses of Psalm 23 are as fresh as if they were written this morning. Theologians E. R. Conder and W. Clarkson wrote,

> "The verses have made themselves at home in every language. They have calmed many fears, dried many tears, soothed many hurts, and provided encouragement to many grief-stricken hearts. The words of Psalm 23 touch, inspire, and comfort us, not as an echo from three thousand years ago, but as the current voice of a living Friend. A child repeats these verses at his mother's knee. The scholar expounds upon them as the deepest truths of life. The church lifts them to heaven in choruses of a thousand voices. The sick believer finds comfort in the promises, and the dying Christian says, 'This is my song,' cheering himself by its words of faith and courage as he enters the path to the ultimate Promised Land."[6]

How can anyone consider this powerful and beautiful psalm to be outdated? It is still relevant to the complexities of the hearts and minds of people in our twenty-first century contemporary society.

As he wrote these words, David seemed to let his mind wander back to the days when he was a young shepherd boy watching over his father's sheep. Perhaps he remembered the many experiences of watching over the flocks and the great responsibility that had been laid upon him as a keeper of the sheep. With these images fresh in his mind, David wrote metaphorically and allegorically, referring to God as a Shepherd and as a Host.

The words of Psalm 23 are designed to help us live with the same confidence David had, even as we live today with a host of problems, threats, and concerns. We face many things that worry us and cause anxiety, but David's testimony can become our testimony—that we can live with confidence amid the uncertainties of life.

RELATIONSHIP

If you're going to live with confidence, you must develop a rich, strong relationship with God. He is the Shepherd, and we are his sheep. It's crucial to understand the Old Testament image of God. When God is called "the Shepherd of Israel," the term refers to his relationship with the covenant nation, the people of God. They considered him to be their national Shepherd.

In this psalm, however, David seems to break with that original Hebrew view of the term. He says, "God has been like a Shepherd for our nation, Israel. He led our fathers and mothers out of slavery in Egypt, and he led us across the Red Sea, into the wilderness, and to the land of promise. While God has been a Shepherd to our nation, I can also remember some things he has done for *me*. God has opened doors for *me* and made ways for *me* and stood by *me* and took care of *me*." So David writes, "The Lord is not just *our* Shepherd, but he's *my* Shepherd."

Some people have a "business relationship" with God. They operate like they have a contract with him, and each side has responsibilities to perform to make things work. The problem with this approach is that there's very little warmth or affection. We're always making demands on God, which creates an entitlement mentality. This perspective leaves us empty and angry. In contrast, my whole life is spent living in the love and light of my Heavenly Father, full of gratitude and wonder. My walk with him is personal and intimate. I can say anything I want to say, and I invite him to correct me whenever I get off track. I look to him for direction and affection. An arms-length, business relationship doesn't work when times are tough because we quickly get disappointed and walk away. Instead, we need to develop a rich, strong, honest personal connection with God.

If you're going to live with confidence, you've got to have a personal, intimate, vibrant relationship with God so that you can say, "The Lord is *my* Shepherd." As great and as gigantic and global as God is, he is tender and gracious enough to allow me to have a personal relationship with him.

Sometimes when I listen to people talk about God, I shake my head in wonder. I hear some people describe God as "a doctor in a sick room," but they've never really been sick. I hear some of them say that God is "bread in a starving land," but they've never been hungry. And I hear people talking about how God is "a pilot through the storms of life," but they've never trusted him in times of trouble.

However, some of us know God because we've seen him come through for us when we needed him most. When you've been so sick that you had no hope, but you trusted God to heal you—and he did—you know God as your Deliverer.

When you've been down to your last dime, and you trusted God to provide—and he did—you know God as your Jehovah Jireh. And when you've been wandering and hopelessly lost, but God brought you into the light, you can say with new meaning, "I know he's a doctor in a sick room. I know he's bread in a starving land. I know he's a way out of dark places, because I've tried him and found him to be true!"

Years ago a man sent his son away to college. The son came back a few years later with a degree. To prove to his father that he was now a scholar, he entered an oratorical contest. He quoted Psalm 23, eloquently and with perfect diction, perfect grammar, and perfect syntax—everything was right. He won first place, came home, showed his father the trophy and said, "Look, Dad, I won the oratorical contest because I knew the psalm. I knew it backward and forward. I quoted it perfectly."

His father said, "That's good, son. I'm glad to know that your education has helped you to learn the psalm."

"Daddy," the young man boasted, "you can't quote the psalm as well as I can."

"You're right, son," his father smiled. "I'm sure I can't quote it as excellently as you're able to quote it, but here's the difference between you and me, son. You know the psalm, but I know the Shepherd. I've lived a while, and I've seen the hand of God deliver me. I know the Shepherd, and it makes a difference. Some day, you'll understand."

Your relationship with God must be personal. It doesn't count that your grandmother loved Jesus or that your father walked with God. Each of us has to develop our own relationship with him. When you can say, like David, "The Lord is my Shepherd," you're also saying that God has sovereignty over you. A shepherd had the right to tell the sheep what to do and where to go—he alone is sovereign over the movements of the flock. Some of us get confused. We think we should tell God what to do and where to go, but that's not it at all. He's the sovereign, supreme Lord of the universe—we're not. He has the right to call the shots in your life: how you spend your time, how you spend your money, who you marry, where you work, and how you treat your family. Listen and obey. When we follow his leading, everybody wins.

CONTENTMENT

Secondly, David is telling us that if you're going to live with confidence, you've got to understand that God will provide for you out of the vast storehouse of his resources. David tells us, "The Lord is my Shepherd, I shall not want." The second clause implies, "Because God is my Shepherd and I've yielded myself to his control in my life, I shall not want. He'll provide all I need. I can trust him."

One scholar has observed that the first line of the psalm could read, "The Lord is my Shepherd—I've got it made!" That word *want* has a broader meaning than what we assume. When we say the words "not want," we know that it means we will lack nothing, but there's a larger implication. It means that God's gracious supply will have an impact on our outlook child. A cherished dream may have gone up in flames, a hope is shattered, and a cherished relationship is strained or broken. The car may have broken down, or we may have wrecked it by doing something foolish like texting and not paying attention to the road. It really doesn't matter what the cause might be. We all face a deep, black hole of disappointment from time to time, and it can feel overwhelming. Sometimes, we are the people going through the difficulty, but at other times, our pain is vicarious—someone we love is enduring a trying time.

At one time or another, the stresses and strains of life become so great that all of us feel like raising both hands and yelling, "I quit! There's no way I'm going to make it. I'm not going to come out of this. It's over for me!"

What comfort or advice do people need when they have lost hope or are tempted to lose hope? Many times the first thing we do is put our arms around them and say, "Don't worry, the Lord will make a way." Another common piece of advice, the standard textbook answer, is to tell them to pray. James tells us, "The effective, fervent prayer of a righteous man avails much" (James 5:16). Advising people to pray while they're on a bumpy road is wise and helpful. The prayer, however, needs to be more than, "God, get me out of this!" God wants us to learn life's most important lessons from the difficulties we face. Our prayer should be much more reflective than a desire to escape!

A bumpy ride doesn't mean you won't get to where God is trying to take you. One Sunday, several years ago while living and attitude. It's the source of true contentment. When David writes, "I shall not want," many people think he means, "I'll never have any problems. I'll never have any hardships, and I'll never have any difficult issues in life." This is a popular but misguided modern theology commonly called "name it and claim it." It promises that if you belong to God, you can name any blessing and claim any provision, and God is obligated to provide. That's just not the case. Certainly, there are no guarantees in the Bible that he is going to make everybody rich, beautiful, and comfortable. Quite often, the richest blessings come in packages of suffering. Even when we are in trouble—and sometimes, only when we're in trouble—we draw close to God and know him more intimately. That's the greatest blessing of all.

David knew what it was like to face hardships. He experienced anguish of soul and faced excruciating difficulties. Sometimes they were so severe that he had to cry in the midnight hour for God to come to his rescue. So when David writes, "I shall not want," he's not implying, "If I trust God, I'll never have any problems, and I'll never have any heartaches." No, what he is saying is that, like Paul, "I have learned the secret of being content in plenty and in want, trusting in the care of God to provide for me. Because I trust God, I can experience his grace and peace in any situation."

There's a difference—a big difference—between happiness and contentment. Happiness is contingent upon a person's happenings. If we are in pleasant surroundings, if we have plenty of money, if people shower affection on us, and if we have no pressures, then we can be happy. How often does that happen? But contentment has nothing to do with what's going on in your surroundings. Contentment is peace in the middle of the storm, joy when things are bad, and hope when life looks hopeless. It's not contingent on external conditions; it's an inner strength that can say, "I don't have the house I want, but it's all right. I don't drive the car I desire, but I'm content. I may not make the money I want to make or have the job I want to have, but I'm trusting God so I'm at peace. God is still able to take care of me, and my contentment is found in him." Contentment is a satisfaction that's rooted in God himself, not our positions, possessions, or popularity. David tells us, "We can be content when we know the Lord is our Shepherd."

Because his resources are available to us, we can be calm. David explains, "He makes me to lie down in green pastures." Sheep are strange animals. It's almost impossible to make sheep lie down. Philip Keller, who is a shepherd and a theologian, suggests that in order for sheep to be made to lie down, four things must be present.

1. They have to be free from fear. They have to know that predators aren't crouching nearby, ready to devour them.
2. They had to be free from friction among the flock. They need peaceful, cordial relationships with the other sheep, with no fighting or competition.
3. They had to be free from pests. If fleas, nasal flies, and

other pesky insects bite the sheep and irritate them, and they won't lie down.

4. Lastly, they had to be free from hunger. As long as they're well fed, they're willing to lie down.

Only a skilled and attentive shepherd can create an environment where the sheep are free from fear, free from friction, free from pests, and free from hunger. David reflected on God's care for him and wrote, "The Lord makes me lie down in green pastures. God creates the right environment. He removes my fears, he removes the friction, he removes the things that bug me, and he satisfies my hunger so I'm able to lie down in peace."

When you know the Shepherd, he will calm your fears. He'll get rid of the things that bug you. And he'll satisfy the deepest hungers of your life. However, human beings are very much like sheep. It's hard for us to lie down because we let so many things bother us. In the middle of the hustle and bustle of life, a host of problems pester us, so it's hard for us to lie down and rest in God's care. But when you know the Shepherd, he creates the environment conducive to calm and rest. No matter what's going on or going wrong, you're able to lie down in God's green pastures and be at peace.

PRESENCE

As we've seen, David said if you're going to live with confidence, you must have a personal relationship with God, you must understand that his resources will be provided, and finally, you must also know that God invites you to return to his presence. Sheep have a way of going astray. They nibble and graze looking for the best grass, and quite often, they don't even look up for long periods of time. Before the sheep notices, it has wandered off the path and gotten lost. It nibbled its way away from the shepherd!

Nibbling—that's how the enemy gets us off track. Nibbling at the wrong party. Nibbling at the wrong habits. Nibbling around the wrong people. And before you know it, you've left the Shepherd. The enemy will cause you to nibble on a cigarette. Then you nibble on a joint, and then you nibble on crack. As you keep nibbling, you wander off from crack to jail, and from jail to the grave—all by just nibbling.

David understood firsthand what it meant to go astray. He could remember the time when he was at the palace, but he should have been leading the army in battle. He walked out on the balcony and saw Bathsheba bathing. All he had to do was go back inside the house and forget what he'd seen, but he called for her to come to his bedroom. He had his way with her. Later, he went to the temple, but he couldn't feel the Spirit of God there. It's bad when you go to church and you can't feel the Spirit of God. It took a good friend, Nathan, to confront him about his sin and turn him back to God. Even then, David had a choice. He had enough sense to repent of his sin. In Psalm 51, his beautiful and piercing confession, he asked God, "Create in me a clean heart. Renew within me the right spirit. Restore unto me the joy of your salvation." God forgave him, and that's why he was able to say in Psalm 23, "He restores my soul."

The word *restore* means "to return to the starting point, to take you back, to revitalize, to reinvigorate." Sometimes restoration was needed because a sheep would become what is called "cast down." This is an Old English shepherd's term. A sheep is cast down when it lies down and can't get back up. Phillip Keller writes, "A 'cast down' sheep is a very pathetic sight. Lying on its back, its feet in the air, it flays away frantically struggling to get up, without success. It will bleat out for help in frightened frustration."[7] While lying in that position, gases build up in the sheep's body, cutting off circulation to its legs and feet. When a sheep is lying on its back, with all four legs in the air, it can't right itself and get back on its feet. A cast sheep could die in a matter of hours unless the shepherd rescues it.

Keller explains that a sheep can become cast down in several ways. Sometimes it will lie down next to a little depression in the ground and roll over accidentally into the depression. The more it wiggles and tries to stand on its own, the worse the cast becomes. Other times, a sheep becomes cast down because the wool has grown too long and heavy. When it lies down, it rolls over and can't get up. And of course, sometimes a sheep would become cast down because it gets too fat and lazy.

When we fall into sin, we have a Shepherd who restores us. It doesn't matter what kind of sin. It could be selfishness, cursing, porn, lying, stealing, laziness, gossiping, or adultery. God's forgiveness cleanses us from all sin and puts us back on our feet. Then he massages our spiritual and emotional legs to get the blood flowing again so we become stronger and more nimble. Finally, we're stronger, and we're able to run with the flock. David had a lot in mind when he wrote the simple sentence: "He restores my soul."

Every now and then we find ourselves in the cast position, on our backs and unable get up. We want to quit sinning, but we can't quit. We want to get out of sticky problems, but we can't escape. The more we try on our own, the worse things get. But we have a Shepherd who comes along and restores us and puts us back on our feet. Once restored, we're put back onto the path of righteousness. If we try to go the wrong way, the Shepherd will stand in the path and say, "You can't go this way. Instead, go that way."

Aren't you glad that God sometimes gets in your way to block your path when you're wandering away from the green pastures? Aren't you glad that there are some things that God won't let you do and some people God won't let you hook up with?

But why would God do that? Why doesn't God get tired of our waywardness and give up on us? Why doesn't God send us to hell? The answer is simple. David said that God's motivation to be a Good Shepherd is "for his name's sake." It's like he's saying, "I can't let you do evil, destructive things because you'd dishonor my name, and my name is too important for me to allow you to damage it."

Isaiah wrote to remind the people of God—including you and me—about the confidence we can have in God, "Have you not known, have you not heard the everlasting God, the Lord, the Creator of the ends of the earth, neither faints nor is weary? His understanding is unsearchable; he gives power to the weak. And to those who have no might, he increases strength. Even the youths, shall faint and be weary, and the young men shall utterly fall, but those who wait on the Lord shall renew their strength, they shall mount up with wings like eagles, they shall run and not be weary, they shall walk and not faint" (Isaiah 40:28-31).

I thank God that I have a Shepherd who doesn't give up on me. If I fall down, he will restore my soul. If I can't get up, he'll put me back on my feet. Then he leads me in the right way. His grace, love, and strength give me confidence!

CHAPTER 10

VICTORY IN THE VALLEY

Surely goodness and mercy shall follow me

All the days of my life;

And I will dwell in the house of the Lord .

Forever. —Psalm 23:6

I know I'm telling my age when I confess to watching Bozo the Clown on television during my childhood. The show aired in our area at 3:30 every afternoon. I couldn't wait to watch it. I loved the show, but—and sometimes there's a *but* when it comes to something we want—I was terrified of the show that aired just before it. The program, Dark Shadows, terrified me with scenes of werewolves, zombies, ghosts, witches, and monsters of every kind. It scared me so much that I waited in the other room while my friends watched the show!

Are you fighting dark shadows today? Are there things that haunt your memory or monsters from the past that frighten you? Dark shadows can appear when we least expect them, when times are good and when times are bad, when the bank account is full and when it's empty. We may be expecting a glorious time in our lives, but—and remember there's always a *but* when it comes to something we want—dark shadows can appear and threaten to ruin our lives.

It doesn't do any good to close our eyes and act like the dark shadows aren't really there. We have to acknowledge them and then push through them. We may want to live on the mountaintop, but valleys are as common as mountains. We have to persevere through the valley. Running away doesn't solve anything. It's not what happens *to you*, but it's how you *perceive* what happens to you that determines the proper response to what happens to you.

Valleys are elongated depressions in the surface of the earth. Wherever there are two or more mountains that are close together, a valley is sandwiched between them. The same principle holds true in our lives. Whenever we enjoy mountains of success and joy, there will subsequently and periodically be some valleys. The terrain of life is not smooth and unchanging. It's a series of highs and lows, good days and bad days. We may wish our lives would be a continuous mountaintop experience of happiness and bliss, but life always includes its fair share of trial, trouble, difficulty and hardship. In fact, for every mountain range, we find valleys on both sides.

All of us experience times in valleys. No matter who you are—your race, your age, your gender, your economic status, or where you are on the social totem pole—every one of us will have to deal with valleys: times of trial, trouble, testing, and tribulation. Sometimes, life seems to be caving in on you, and death and destruction are in your immediate destiny. There will be times when pain and problems invade your space. Sometimes, it seems like joy has lost your address, peace has forgotten your phone number, and the automobile of your happiness has run out of gas. Every one of us has to deal with valleys in life.

- Problems on the job—that's a valley.
- Problems in the home—that's a valley.
- Children in trouble—that's a valley.
- Parents don't understand you—that's a valley.
- You lose a loved one—that's a valley.
- You can't find a job—that's a valley.
- You find yourself having suicidal moments—that's a valley.
- You get sick in your body—that's a valley.

So, how do we find victory in the valley? Let's look at three things that determine how we claim our victory: progression, perception, and protection.

PROGRESSION

First of all, you have got to get moving and keep moving. Sitting still only leaves you perpetually stuck in the same place. Remember the old Nike ad campaign, "Just do it." That sums up an important spiritual principle: You've got to get moving.

In Psalm 23:4, David wrote, "Yea, though I walk...." Walking implies movement, progression, and going somewhere. The worst thing you could ever do in your valley is to stop moving. Let's be honest. When things aren't going the way we hoped, it's easy for us to sit down and have a pity party. We invite everybody to come to our party, and then we complain and grumble and gripe.

If you choose to wallow in self-pity, you'll become a *victim* of your valley, rather than being a *victor* in your valley. If you're going to be victorious, whatever you do, *don't stop walking* and *don't stop moving.*

- You may wonder how bills are going to get paid, but while you wonder, keep walking.
- You may wonder how you're going to get your finances together, but while you wonder, keep walking.
- You may wonder how what's going to happen to your marriage, but while you wonder, keep walking.
- You may wonder how what's going to happen to you now that you've gotten the diagnosis of a terminal disease, but while you wonder, keep walking.

If you keep walking you might discover the same thing that Mary discovered after Jesus died: When she got to the tomb, the angel had already rolled the stone away, and she saw the Lord! In her valley of grief, she didn't stop moving.

PERCEPTION

David says, "The reason I'm going to be victorious in my valley is because I have a right perception of what's happening to me." He was unflinchingly optimistic. No matter what the Lord asked, David answered, "Yes."

If you're going to be victorious, you need to perceive life from God's point of view. Yes, it's dark and dangerous in the valley. David wondered whether or not he would come out alive, but when he stepped back and looked at all the things that were happening, he gained a new perception. He looked at the darkness, the danger and all the hardships, and he came to the conclusion, "You know what? These are nothing but shadows."

Shadows look dark and dangerous. They appear sinister, so they can easily intimidate you, but in reality, a shadow can't harm you. The shadow of a snake can't bite you, and the shadow of a lion can't attack you. If you don't look at things properly, the shadow of a snake or a lion can make you run away. It all depends on how you see things.

Sometimes what seems to be the *end* of the road is only a *bend* in the road. You look at your life now, and it looks so hopeless. But the life of faith says it's not the end of the road, it's just a bend in the road. God has much more for you, if you'll just keep going. To get through the valley, you must acknowledge the reality of the situation—not shadows, but substance.

Second, if you're going to be victorious in those valley times, you've got to announce your response in the valley. How you respond to the valley determines whether or not you'll be victorious. To respond with bold faith, make declarations while you are going through the valley. Use the words of Scripture to banish fear and doubt.

When we're in our valleys, it's easy to become afraid and allow ourselves to be victimized by anxiety and worry. The only thing that can cancel out fear is faith. Faith and fear are like light and darkness—they can't occupy the same space at the same time. When you're walking into a dark room and turn the light on, light comes in but darkness has to leave.

When my girls were little, they would come into our room and say, "Mommy, Daddy, I can't sleep."

I would inquire, "What's the matter, Marcie? What's wrong, Jessica? Why can't you sleep?"

"It's dark in my room. Can I get into bed with you?"

"Come on," we'd say and they would crawl into bed with us.

Picture the scene: These little girls got up in their dark room, walked down a dark hall, came into our dark room, climbed into bed, and went to sleep. What's the difference? Why could they sleep with us but not alone in their room? Because they knew their daddy and mommy were with them.

When you are in your valley and it's dark, you can survive if you remember that God is with you. He's "as near as our breath." David says that he's not going to be afraid because God is with him.

Last, we must declare our final outcome. David says. "Yea, though I walk *through* the valley." He admits he's in the valley now, but he makes the bold declaration that he's going to come out of it. He didn't say, "Yea, though I *sit* in the valley."

No, he says he's walking through it. If you keep picking up your feet and putting them down, you're going to come out on the other side.

Your valley may be dark, but you've got to declare your final outcome, while you're still going through it. You've got to tell yourself, "I'm going to get through this."

- It's a dark valley, but I'm going to get through this.
- It's a heavy burden, but I'm going to get through this.
- It's a tough time, but I'm going to get through this.
- It's a financial crisis, but I'm going to get through this.
- It's a lonely night, but I'm going to get through this.
- I can't find a job, but I'm going to get through this.
- I need a door opened, and I'm going to get through it.
- I need a miracle, and God is going to give me one.

Running from the reality of our valleys short circuits the power of God to transform our lives and prevents us from learning important lessons. In his book, *The Healing Path*, psychologist Dan Allender describes the spiritual perception we can have about even the most painful events in our lives. He wrote,

> "If we fail to anticipate thoughtfully how we will respond to the harm of living in a fallen world, the pain may be for naught. It will either numb or destroy us rather than refine and even bless us.... Healing in this life is not the resolution of our past; it is the use of our past to draw us into deeper relationship with God and his purposes for our lives."[8]

Dark valleys are very real, but the unseen is more real than the seen. God's goodness and power cancel the darkness and overcome the enemy's schemes. Learn to put on a new pair of spiritual lenses and see the valley the way God sees it.

PROTECTION

To experience victory in the valley of low moments of your life, you must acknowledge the reality of your valley. Accept your resources in the valley. David wrote, "Thy rod and thy staff, they comfort me."

The rod was a club-like stick that the shepherd used to fight off predators—wolves, cougars and coyotes that would attack the sheep. One of the resources that we have in our valley is God's protection. Sheep are harmless, but they're also defenseless. They depend totally on the shepherd for their protection. David understood this truth from first-hand experiences. As a young boy, a bear and a lion attacked his father's sheep. David put his life on the line to protect the sheep. He killed the lion and the bear because a good shepherd will lay down his life for the sheep.

God will protect you and fight for you. Since Barack Obama was elected our 44th President of the United States, he has had more death threats than any president in the history of our nation. When asked if he feared for his personal safety, he replied, "No, I'm not afraid because of two reasons. First, because of my Secret Service protection, but also because of my faith in God."

The president values his Secret Service protection, but he's got something more than that—he's got angelic protection. Old folks where I was raised sometimes said, "All night and all day, the angels keep watching over me."

We have God's protection, and we also have his assurance. David not only mentions the rod, but also the staff. The staff was a long stick, sometimes with a crook on the end. The shepherd used the staff to count the sheep. He kept a detailed record of his sheep, and when the numbers didn't add up, he knew that a sheep was either lost or had fallen into a ditch. If one was missing, he went looking for it. If he found the sheep in the ditch and it couldn't get out, he reached down with the crooked end, hooked it under its shoulders, and lifted it out of the ditch.

The assurance we have is that the Lord our Shepherd keeps a watchful eye over us. If we fall into the ditch of despair, God will come and pull us out.

We also have favor. David wrote, "You prepare a table before me in the presence of my enemies." In the summer, shepherds led the sheep up into the high country to find better grazing. In the mountain were long ledges called tablelands. That had rich, lush grass on the top, and the shepherd led the sheep there they could graze. Wolves, bears, and lions lived down in the valley, but they couldn't get to the tablelands because the shepherd was keeping a watchful eye on them.

David wrote about God's care: "You prepare a tableland for me in the presence of my enemies." In other words, when God is your Shepherd, he'll bless you in front of your enemies, and there's not a thing your enemies can do about it. That's called favor! When God gives you favor, he'll make your enemies your footstool. When God gives you favor, people on at work who tried to keep you from getting a promotion will be moved out of the way, and God will grant you the promotion.

David then shifts metaphors to explain the comfort and refreshment God gives: "You anoint my head with oil." David sees God now, not as the Shepherd, but as a gracious Host who invites people to a grand banquet. In the East in the ancient world, when a host welcomed people to a banquet, he anointed them with oil to honor them, to give them comfort, and to extend hospitality. Our Good Shepherd and Host welcomes us to the banquet of his grace to honor us as his beloved children, comforts us as we walk with him, and warmly accepts us at his table of love. The oil is the Holy Spirit, the Comforter, who comes alongside us to give encouragement and aid in our times of need. The Holy Spirit lifts up bowed down heads and eases troubled minds. He mends broken hearts.

When you're down, look up and thank God because we have a Comforter who will lift us up. And someday, he will lift us up to dwell in his house forever! The Good Shepherd doesn't invite us to be a guest for only a single banquet meal or an isolated day of blessing. That would be more than we deserve, but his grace is far better than that. One day in the presence of his glory would be magnificent, but God, the Gracious Host, invites us to be his guest for eternity.

In these pages, we've *walked* through our valley to experience God's care even in the most difficult times in our lives. Read Psalm 23 again, but with an emphasis on the personal pronouns:

"The Lord is *my* Shepherd.

I shall not want.

He makes *me* to lie down in green pastures.

He leads *me* beside the still waters. He restores *my* soul. He leads *me* in paths of righteousness for his name's sake.

Yea, though *I* walk through the valley of the shadow of death,

I will fear no evil.

You are with *me*,

Your rod and your staff they comfort *me*.

You prepare a table before *me*

In the presence of *my* enemies.

You anoint *my* head with oil.

My cup runs over.

Surely goodness and mercy shall follow *me*

All the days of *my* life, and

I will dwell in the house of the Lord forever."

David uses picturesque and allegorical language in this psalm. In the first three verses, he carries us on a journey to some of the mountaintop experiences in his life. He tells us that on the mountaintop with his Shepherd, there was no need for him to worry about those things that were needed for his survival. The Lord supplied all he needed.

On the mountaintop with his Shepherd, David was led into places of peace, prosperity, and tranquility—places where the pastures are green and the waters are still. But as David continues to look back over his life and his many experiences, he makes an announcement that reminds us that life not only affords us the opportunity to enjoy the glitter of the mountain, but we have to deal with the gloom of the valley.

From time to time, all of us have to deal with lonesome valleys. We don't want to be there, but wishing them away only creates darker shadows. We have to face the reality of our valleys so that we look to God for peace, pardon, and purpose while we're there.

I know there's a theology that says you should never admit the negative things that happen in your life, that you should never even speak about those things—admit you're sick, confess that you're in trouble, or say that you're having hard times—because to speak those things, they say, means you're not living in faith. They reason, "Death and life are in the power of the tongue." But a life of faith is not a life of denial. I can admit that I'm sick in my body and still believe that God is Jehovah Rapha, the God of healing.

We shouldn't live in denial; the valleys we experience are real. The valley is dark and the way is rough, but in the midst of our valleys, we don't have to be afraid—we can go to the Shepherd and tell him about our troubles.

In the bad times, we can follow the profound advice of a well-known song:

"Now let us have a little talk with Jesus.
Let us tell Him all about our troubles.
He will hear our faintest cry
And He will answer by and by.
Now when you feel a little prayer wheel turning,
Then you'll know a little fire is burning.
You will find a little talk with Jesus makes it right."[9]

Even in a valley, we are reminded that if we have the Lord as our Shepherd, that he can give us victory in our valleys. We just have to keep walking through the dark shadows. That's how we experience God's comfort in the crazy seasons of life.

Keep looking up.

ENDNOTES

1 From "Portraits," In Touch Ministries, www.intouch.org/myintouch/mighty/portraits/corrie_ten_boom

2 Philip Yancey, *Reaching for the Invisible God,* (Zondervan, Grand Rapids, Michigan, 2000), p. 69.

3 J. I. Packer, *Knowing God,* (Intervarsity Press, Downer's Grove, Ill., 1973), p. 227.

4 Dr. Richard Swenson, *Margin: Restoring Emotional, Physical, Financial and Time Reserves to Our Overloaded Lives,* (Navpress, Colorado Springs, 2004).

5 Charles Swindoll, "An Appraisal," Insight for Living, September 26, 2009.

6 E. R. Conder and W. Clarkson, *The Pulpit Commentary* (Grand Rapids, MI: Eerdmans, 1978), 164.

7 Phillip Keller, *A Shepherd's Look at Psalm 23,* (Zondervan, Grand Rapids, 2007), p. 58.

8 Dan Allender, *The Healing Path,* (Water Brook Press, Colorado Springs, Colorado, 1999), pp. 5-6.

9 "Just a Little Talk with Jesus," Words and Music by Cleavant Derricks, 1937.

ABOUT THE AUTHOR

Dr. Maurice Watson is the Senior Pastor of Beulahland Bible Church, located in Macon, Georgia. He was the seventh of eight children born in Little Rock, Arkansas. At the age of 16, he accepted the call to preach the gospel, and two years later he was ordained.

Dr. Watson received a Bachelor of Arts Degree in Education from Philander Smith College in Little Rock and was class Valedictorian. He earned a Masters Degree in Theology at Creighton University in Omaha, Nebraska, and a Doctor of Ministry Degree from Beeson Divinity School in Birmingham, Alabama.

His first pastorate was at St. Mark Baptist Church in Little Rock, where he served for seven years. In November 1988, he accepted the call to pastor the Salem Baptist Church in Omaha, Nebraska, where he served for 15 years.

In early 2004, sensing a new call of God on his life, Dr. Maurice Watson accepted the senior pastorate of Beulahland Bible Church in Macon, Georgia, with the vision and strategy

of impacting the world from Middle Georgia. His leadership took Beulahland to a second location of worship in Warner Robins, Georgia, in February 2005.

Dr. Watson's vision of "faith on the fast track" didn't stop there. Under his leadership, the church constructed a second worship facility on its Macon campus. The membership now enjoys a state-of-the-art 2500 seat sanctuary.

He also has a dynamic itinerant preaching ministry that extends across the continent and the globe.

Dr. Watson is married to his wife, Janice, and they have two beautiful daughters.

In addition to his pastoral calling, Dr. Watson also has a dynamic preaching ministry that extends across the continent and around the globe. He has been described as one of the premier preachers of our generation and is sought after for his Spirit-anointed and Biblically sound proclamation of God's Word. He regularly speaks in churches and at conferences.

Dr. Watson is motivated by his love for people, his love for preaching, and his belief that no one is beyond God's reach. "I was born—put on this Earth in this Universe—to be a preacher, teacher, and pastor of people. Seeing lives transformed through the clear, compelling teaching of God's truth continually motivates me. It's my purpose for being alive."

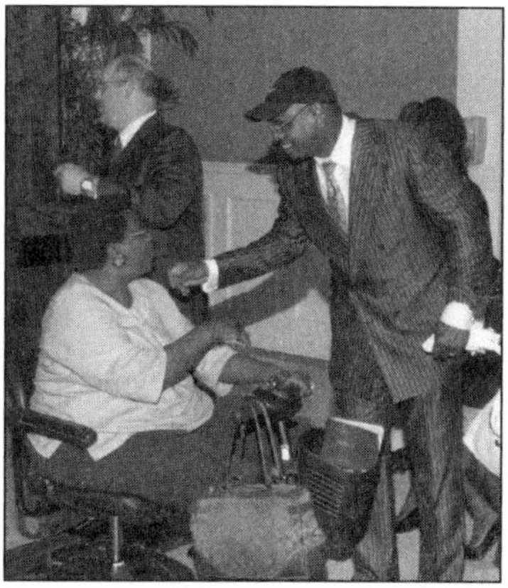

For more information about available dates and topics:

Go online to www.beulahland.org

Or call (478) 784-1555 ext 210

RESOURCES

To order more copies of this book, and for information about volume discounts and shipping, go to **www.beulahland.org**

Dr. Watson also offers a wide range of messages in CD and DVD formats, either in sermon series or as stand-alone messages.

To see a list of these messages, go to www.beulahland.org and click on "Bookstore."